GEORGE HERBERT

By the same author
THE DIVINE IMAGE, a study of Blake's interpretation of Christianity: Edizioni di Storia e Letteratura, Rome, 1950.

With Ronald Bottrall
COLLECTED ENGLISH VERSE, Sidgwick & Jackson, 1946.

GEORGE HERBERT

Drawn by G. Clint, A.R.A., from a contemporary portrait

GEORGE HERBERT

By MARGARET BOTTRALL

LONDON
JOHN MURRAY, ALBEMARLE STREET, W.

First Edition . . . 1954

Printed in Great Britain by
Wyman and Sons, Ltd., London, Fakenham and Reading
and Published by John Murray (Publishers) Ltd.

IN MEMORIAM H. S. S.

Contents

CHAPTER		PAGE
I.	The Layman	1
II.	The Priest	25
III.	Literary Remains	49
IV.	"The Country Parson"	67
V.	Herbert's Themes	83
VI.	Herbert's Craftsmanship	99
VII.	Literary Affinities	117
VIII.	The Christian Poet	134

Prefatory Note

FOR the text of Herbert's writings I have used F. E. Hutchinson's edition of his *Works* (Oxford, 1941), and the page references following quotations are always to that edition. I have made extensive use of the biographical and bibliographical material set out by Canon Hutchinson in his admirable edition, and I have also used G. H. Palmer's three-volume edition of Herbert's *English Works* (Houghton Mifflin, 1915).

I have drawn so liberally on Walton's *Life of Mr. George Herbert* that to save footnotes I have given page references to the World's Classics edition of Walton's *Lives* immediately after each extract.

Some of the material in Chapter IV was used in a talk on George Herbert's *Country Parson*, broadcast in the Third Programme of the B.B.C. in March 1952.

I should like to thank Dr. Bernard Blackstone for letting me read his unpublished thesis on *George Herbert's Thought and Imagery*, which gave me the impetus to get down to work on this study. My thanks are also due to Mr. Edmund Blunden for permission to quote from his translation of one of Herbert's Latin poems, and to Messrs. Chatto & Windus for permission to quote from Miss Rosemary Freeman's *English Emblem Books*.

The frontispiece portrait of George Herbert, from a print by E. White, is reproduced by kind permission of the Librarian and Fellows of Trinity College, Cambridge. It appeared as frontispiece to the 1640 edition of *The Temple*.

M. B.

Thaxted, 1953.

I

The Layman

GEORGE HERBERT can hardly be reckoned as a major poet, because the scale of his work is so small. His fame rests on one brief volume of poems and a little treatise on the life of a country parson. All his poems are on sacred themes, and nearly all are lyrical. But if a distinction can profitably be drawn between "major" and "great", Herbert surely deserves recognition as a great poet, in the same sense as Nicholas Hilliard was a great miniaturist. In point of workmanship it is not always the major artists who are the most accomplished. Herbert was an exquisite craftsman, though he had not the reserves of creative energy or the soaring imagination needful for work on a grand scale. His greatness lies in the way he handles great concepts. God's love for mankind, man's ingratitude; the longing of the soul for spiritual comfort, the satisfaction of that longing; these are Herbert's themes, and there are none greater. Though his manner of treating them is often familiar, it is never trivial. He orders his ideas with power as well as reverence, neither inflating himself nor diminishing them.

Too often his poetry is assessed as though it were the work of a minor metaphysical, one of Donne's disciples. Certainly Donne was a figure familiar to George Herbert from his schooldays onwards, and he had unusual opportunities for studying his poems; but the younger man had his own theories of how to write, theories which link him more closely with Sidney than with Donne. Besides, the whole cast of his

George Herbert

mind was radically different from Donne's. He had as great a capacity for faith as Donne had for doubt and experiment. It is strange that a man with so marked a distaste for speculative thought should ever have been labelled "metaphysical". Herbert's wit was fired not by the example of Donne but by the paradoxical nature of Christianity itself.

His poems mirror his temperament and tastes with singular clarity; and *The Country Parson*, though not autobiographical, tells us much about his attitude towards his fellow-men, to his church and to the mysteries of his faith. From his surviving letters to relatives and friends we get further insight into his character. His life and family background, too, are unusually well documented, so that lovers of Herbert have every reason to feel that they know him intimately.

There was only one major crisis in his life, and it came late, only three years before he died of consumption at the age of forty. Until that time, Herbert had led a privileged, easy and agreeable life. Fortune had denied him only one important gift—good health. In every other way he was remarkably favoured. Besides possessing an exceptional mind, good looks and great charm, he had powerful family connections, a brilliant and devoted mother, a happy home, an excellent education and many friends. Though he was far from rich, he was never exposed to hardship, nor had he to struggle from obscurity to a place in the sunshine. At no time did he abuse his privileges, conforming always to the high standards set before a gentleman and scholar nurtured in the ways of Christian behaviour; but nobody encountering George Herbert, the young Public Orator of Cambridge, intent upon making a good impression on King James I, could have prophesied that he would end his days as the venerated priest of a small country parish.

For years he had vacillated, distracted from the study of divinity by opportunities to shine in university office

The Layman

and at court, and reluctant to commit himself to the irrevocable decision of taking holy orders, though this had been in his mind since boyhood. When at last he did surrender his whole life and being to God and was ordained priest, he was transformed; his infirmity of purpose vanished. Not all his innermost hesitations and fears were ended; but he devoted his whole intellectual and spiritual energy, all his gifts and graces, to a single end—the service of his divine Master. The intensity with which he pursued this end made a profound impression on those who knew him. Though he was a country parson for less than three years, he was esteemed by the people around Salisbury as little less than sainted. Country folk are commonly suspicious of newcomers, and it takes a great deal to make Englishmen testify to anyone's holiness; but they recognize a saint when they see one, and they saw one in the rector of Bemerton.

No institution is more baffling to outsiders than the Church of England, but its very illogicality and eclecticism commend it to many English minds, and in its endeavour to maintain a middle course and to exercise tolerance of judgment it chimes with something very central in the English spirit. George Herbert had the good fortune to be born and bred in it at a time when it was enjoying a spell of rare equilibrium and was well able to answer the needs of devout men and women who did not wish to renounce either the whole Catholic heritage or their own intellectual liberty. Herbert found its *via media* exactly to his liking. In some respects, his glad adherence to the Anglican church limited his poetic range; but it gave him a compensatory strength, the strength of a man who has a spiritual home in which he finds himself happy and at peace.

Though all Herbert's poems are religious, and the majority of them written towards the end of his life, the whole of his poetry is enriched by the variegated pattern of his experiences

George Herbert

before he became a priest. The easy assurance of his style reminds us that he had long been accustomed to "trade in courtesies and wit". His musicianship is everywhere apparent, and no less pervasive, though much less obvious, is the influence of his classical studies. His avoidance of allusions to pagan mythology is of course deliberate; but behind his highly developed literary discrimination lie years of familiarity with writers who exalted decorum, elegance and sobriety; years, too, of practice in the writing of Latin and Greek verse.

Reading Herbert's poems we are constantly reminded that he had cultivated

> "the pliant mind, whose gentle measure
> Complies and suits with all estates."
> *(Content*, p. 69.)

His command of the right tone and manner for whatever occasion never fails him; and his fastidious taste prevents his religious verse from lapsing into mawkishness or contorting itself into ill-judged extravagances. His was a disciplined mind and a finely tempered spirit; and with this inner integrity went an extreme sensitiveness. Though a far less passionate man than Donne, he was scarcely less subject to variableness of mood, and was certainly no less interested in scrutinizing and recording his own feelings.

* * *

George Herbert came of distinguished stock. His father's family had for generations been famous on the borders of Wales for their gallantry and enterprise. An elder branch had been ennobled with the earldom of Pembroke, and a strong cousinly feeling prevailed between them and the Montgomery Herberts. George was born on April 3rd, 1593,

The Layman

either at Montgomery Castle, the residence of his grandfather, or else at the adjacent Black Hall. He was the fifth son of Richard and Magdalen Herbert. His father, described by his son Edward[1] as "black-haired and bearded ... of a manly or somewhat stern look, but withal very handsome, and well compact in his limbs, and of a great courage", was a landowner, respected for his just dealings. He died when George was only three years old. There were already six sons and three daughters, and Magdalen Herbert bore a seventh son shortly after the death of her husband.

She was, fortunately, a woman of outstanding intelligence and courage, and she bent all her energies to the task of rearing these ten children to take their rightful places in the world. For a while after her husband's death, Mrs. Herbert went to live with her widowed mother, Lady Newport, at Eyton in Shropshire. The Newports were rich Shropshire landowners, and Lady Newport was well known for her piety and liberality. In order, however, to give the children greater educational opportunities than they would have had in the marches of Wales, Mrs. Herbert took a house in Oxford.

By all accounts she was an exceptionally gracious, good and generous-hearted woman; but her maternal devotion may have been slightly overwhelming, in spite of Izaak Walton's careful assertions to the contrary. George, though deeply attached to her, calls her *severa parens*; and there are indications in Edward Herbert's *Autobiography* that he did not greatly appreciate her foresight in marrying him, while he was still a student at Oxford, to a cousin considerably older than himself, in order to keep him out of mischief. Though Mrs. Herbert entered her eldest son at University College and provided him with "a fit Tutor ... yet she continued there

[1] *Autobiography* of Lord Herbert of Cherbury, ed. Sidney Lee, 2nd ed. Routledge, 1906, p. 2.

with him, and still kept him in a moderate awe of herself: and so much under her own eye, as to see and converse with him daily; but she managed this power over him without any such rigid sourness, as might make her company a torment to her Child; but with such a sweetness and complyance with the recreations and pleasures of youth, as did incline him willingly to spend much of his time in the company of his dear and careful Mother".[1]

Edward rewarded her devotion by becoming an able courtier and diplomatist, a remarkably independent philosopher and a considerable poet; but in his autobiography he actually devotes more space and warmer praise to his grandmother, Lady Newport, than to his mother. The most probable reason to account for his very brief mention of her is that after twelve years of widowhood, when she was nearly forty, she married a man much the same age as her eldest son. The marriage, moreover, was a conspicuously happy one.

Against Edward Herbert's grudging attitude must be set John Donne's many tributes of affection and esteem. He probably became acquainted with Mrs. Herbert about 1604, when she moved from Oxford to London. Walton says that they got to know one another at Oxford, but his account contains some errors of fact, though it faithfully reflects the spirit of the friendship that sprang up between them. It lasted some twenty years, surviving Mrs. Herbert's marriage to Sir John Danvers, and coming to an end only with her death. She was eight years older than Donne, and enjoyed a much more secure social position. She helped and encouraged him at a time when, newly and imprudently married, he was hard put to it to earn a living; and he repaid her with lasting devotion and with friendship towards her children as well as herself.

---

[1] Walton, *Life of Mr. George Herbert*, World's Classics, p. 264.

The Layman

It is to Donne that we owe the delightful picture of Sunday evenings in the Herbert household, when Mrs. Herbert "with her whole family ... did ... shut up the day, at night, with a generall, with a cheerful *singing of Psalmes*; this Act of cheerfulnesse, was still the last Act of that Family, united in it selfe, and with God".[1] Though a devout woman, Mrs. Herbert was not unworldly, and delighted to entertain her friends. "Her house," says Donne, "was a court in conversation of the best." Her charity and courtesy were unfailing, and moderation was her rule in all things. It is not fanciful to connect George Herbert's love of order and his infallible sense of what is appropriate with the influence exercised by his mother. She had great personal beauty too. Donne says, "God gave her such a comelinesse as, though she was not proud of it, yet she was so content with it as not to go about to mend it by any art ... As for her attire, it was never sumptuous, never sordid; but always agreeable to her quality and agreeable to her company." Her beauty, moreover, did not fade with the years. It was for Magdalen Herbert that Donne wrote the Elegy known as *The Autumnal*, with its famous opening lines:

> No *Spring*, nor *Summer* Beauty hath such grace,
> As I have seen in one Autumnall face.[2]

In another poem addressed to her he uses the lovely phrase "her warm redeeming hand".[3]

We know from Walton that Donne in 1607 sent a set of sacred poems to Mrs. Herbert with a dedicatory sonnet on Mary Magdalene. Whether they were the sonnet-sequence

---

[1] Funeral Sermon, quoted in Appendix of Sidney Lee's edition of Lord Herbert's *Autobiography*. Other quotations on this page from same source.

[2] *Poems*, ed. H. J. C. Grierson, p. 92.

[3] ibid., p. 216.

George Herbert

La Corona or other "Hymns now lost to us" is a matter of conjecture:[1] but we may be sure that George Herbert, while still a boy, was privileged to read in manuscript the poems that Donne used to send to his mother for her approval.

He was exceptionally fortunate in his mother and in his home; but Mrs. Herbert did not try to keep him under her wing, for she was a woman ambitious for her sons. His brother Charles had been sent to Winchester, and George, when he reached the age of twelve, left the tutor who had been teaching him and his younger brothers at home, and went to Westminster School. The actual date of his admission is not given in the school records; he may have continued to live under his mother's roof for his first school year, but after that he was nominated a King's Scholar, which involved residence in the school.

According to Walton, young George was even now destined for sainthood. "The beauties of his pretty behaviour and wit, shin'd and became so eminent and lovely in this his innocent age, that he seem'd to be marked out for piety, and to become the care of Heaven, and of a particular good Angel to guard and guide him" (p. 262). This is the kind of retrospective tribute that very easily gets paid to a venerated man without supporting evidence; but certainly as a King's Scholar at Westminster George Herbert had every opportunity to develop that love of the Anglican church and its liturgy which he expressed so warmly in maturity.

The headmaster of Westminster at that time was Richard Ireland, and the reputation of the school was high, especially in classical studies, to which George Herbert evidently applied himself diligently. Even as a boy, he was somewhat handicapped by delicate health, as we can gather from the head-

---

[1] Donne, *The Divine Poems*, ed. Helen Gardner, Oxford, 1952, p. 55. For an account of the friendship between Mrs. Herbert and Donne, see an article by Dr. H. W. Garrod in *Review of English Studies*, xxi, 1945.

The Layman

master's parting exhortation to him and John Hacket (later Bishop of Coventry and Lichfield), when they had just gained their elections to Trinity College, Cambridge. Ireland said that "he expected to have credit by *them two* at the University, or would never hope for it afterwards by any while he lived: and added withal, that he need give them no counsel to follow their Books, but rather to study moderately and use exercise; their parts being so good, that if they were careful not to impair their health with too much study, they would not fail to arrive at the top of learning in any *Art* or *Science*".[1] Within a few months of his proceeding to Cambridge, however, we find George Herbert in a letter to his mother complaining of "my late Ague"; and in subsequent letters, as well as in his poems, he speaks frequently of the trials of ill-health.

His mother's second marriage took place when George Herbert was still a schoolboy at Westminster, and all the evidence goes to show that he and his young step-father were on the best of terms. Aubrey, whose grandmother was a Danvers, has a good deal to say about Sir John. Of the marriage itself he speaks in disapproving terms; it displeased Sir John's brother, the Earl of Danby, that a rich and handsome young man should marry a woman old enough to be his mother. "He married her for love of her Witt," says Aubrey. "Twas Sir John Danvers of Chelsey ... who first taught us the way of Italian Gardens: He had well travelled France and Italy, and made good Observations: He had in a faire Body an harmonicall Mind: in his Youth his Complexion was so exceedingly beautifull and fine that ... the People would come after him in the Street to admire him ... He was a great acquaintance and Favorite of the Lord Chancellor Bacon, who took much delight in that elegant Garden. Sir

[1] Quoted by F. E. Hutchinson from J. Hacket, *A Century of Sermons*, 1675. Life by T. Plume, p.v. Herbert's *Works*, p. xxv.

George Herbert

John, being my Relation and faithfull Friend, was wont in fair mornings in the Summer to brush his Beaver-hatt on the Hyssop and Thyme, which did perfume it with its naturall Spirit, and would last a morning, or longer."[1] To the fifteen-year-old George this charming young man must have been much more like an elder brother than a step-father; and though when he wrote to him from Cambridge he always addressed him in terms of respect, he clearly regarded him as a friend—almost, on occasion, as a fellow-conspirator.

George Herbert was not yet seventeen when he entered Trinity College, a brilliant boy, of whom great things were expected. To mark the New Year's Day of 1609, the first he spent at Cambridge, he sent his mother two sonnets, declaring his resolve to devote his poetic gifts to sacred themes. To this resolve he remained constant. As far as is known, he wrote no secular poems, apart from a few complimentary Latin pieces. Clearly the bent of his mind was already towards religion; but in those early days it seemed as though he could hope to enjoy the best of both worlds. In one of the most patently autobiographical of his poems, he speaks of his happy boyhood. The paying of due allegiance to God was a joy, and so were the beauties of formal worship; nor did these joys conflict with those derived from his "stock of natural delights"—his lively intellect, his passion for music, his good looks and easy way of life.

> When first thou didst entice to thee my heart,
>   I thought the service brave:
> So many joyes I writ down for my part,
>   Besides what I might have
> Out of my stock of naturall delights,
> Augmented with thy gracious benefits.

---

[1] Aubrey, *Brief Lives*, ed. O. Lawson Dick, Secker & Warburg, 1950, p. 80.

The Layman

> I looked on thy furniture so fine,
>   And made it fine to me:
> Thy glorious household-stuffe did me entwine,
>   And 'tice me unto thee.
> Such starres I counted mine: Both heav'n and earth
> Payd me my wages in a world of mirth . . .
>
> At first thou gav'st me milk and sweetnesses;
>   I had my wish and way:
> My dayes were straw'd with flow'rs and happinesse;
>   There was no moneth but May . . .
>   (*Affliction i*, p. 46.)

George Herbert went up to Cambridge well grounded in the classics; but it was his mother's hope, if Walton is to be believed, that he should pursue the study of divinity and eventually take holy orders. His youthful sonnets suggest that when he began his life as an undergraduate he shared his mother's aspirations; but the Herberts were notoriously an energetic, ambitious and high-spirited clan, who distinguished themselves as soldiers, courtiers, judges and administrators. George had one scholarly brother, Charles, who became a Fellow of New College, dying young; his other brothers were all men of action, and of himself he says:

> Whereas my birth and spirit rather took
>   The way that takes the town;
> Thou didst betray me to a lingring book,
>   And wrap me in a gown.
>   (*Affliction i*, p. 47).

Whether he really found academic life tedious we may doubt, for he quickly made a success of it; and the attraction of university office before very long made him relegate the project of being ordained to second place in his mind.

He was elected a minor Fellow of Trinity in October 1614

George Herbert

and a major Fellow in March 1615/16, taking his Master's degree a few months later. In the following year he was given a minor College office, which involved him in a little teaching, though he had plenty of time to pursue his own studies. It was about this time that he wrote to Sir John Danvers, complaining that for want of money to buy books he is hampered just when he is "setting foot into Divinitie, to lay the platform" of his future life. "And shall I then be fain alwayes to borrow Books, and build on anothers foundation? What Trades-man is there who will set up without his Tools? Pardon my boldness Sir, it is a most serious Case ..." (p. 364). He protests that, in spite of studying thrift, he cannot afford to buy the needful learned tomes, and suggests that his step-father should use his influence with the trustees of the Herbert estate so as to increase his annuity while he is at the university; then, he says, he will cease his "clamorous and greedy bookish requests" (p. 367).

Within a few months, however, he is writing to Danvers in a very different vein, soliciting his help in obtaining the post of Public Orator in the university. Though Herbert made light of suggestions that holding this office might deflect him from the study of divinity, the tone of his letters is not that of an earnest scholar, but of a man who wants to make his mark in the little world of the university and in the great world beyond its confines.

He had already been appointed to his first university post, as Praelector or Reader in Rhetoric, on the foundation of Sir Robert Rede. This brought with it the obligation to lecture four or five mornings a week to first-year students. The lecturer was expected to expound, in English, such famous orators as Cicero or Quintilian; and Herbert incurred some censure, not surprisingly, when he chose to analyse in the most flattering terms a Latin oration of King James. This shows which way his thoughts were veering.

The Layman

Having acted on more than one occasion as deputy to Sir Francis Nethersole, the Public Orator, he was anxious, as soon as he gathered that Nethersole was to relinquish office, to become his successor. The two letters to Sir John Danvers on this topic lend some colour to Charles Cotton's comment that his

> "education,
> Manners, and parts, by high applauses blown,
> Was deeply tainted by ambition."[1]

He was so much attracted by the Public Oratorship that he was quite willing to do a fair amount of intriguing to procure it. He explains to Danvers that the Orator's is "the finest place in the University, though not the gainfullest; . . . for the Orator writes all the University Letters, makes all the Orations, be it to King, Prince, or whatever comes to the University; to requite these pains, he takes place next to the Doctors, is at all their Assemblies and Meetings, and sits above the Proctors . . . and such like Gaynesses, which will please a young man well" (p. 369).

While he asks his step-father to use his influence with powerful people in London, Herbert frankly admits that he hopes to "work the heads" of the colleges to his purpose, and adds: "I hope I shall get this place without all your London helps . . . that you may see, if all fail, yet I am able to stand on mine own legs" (p. 370). He was, in any case, taking no chances. Whether as a result of his own efforts or of combined operations, he was elected to the Public Oratorship in January 1619.

Though a young man, he was eminently well fitted for the post, having the advantages of fine breeding and courtly

---

[1] *To my Old, and most Worthy Friend, Mr. Izaak Walton,* included in 1675 edition of Walton's *Lives.*

manners as well as good scholarship. During his first year of office he was very active, and the letters and speeches extant show his ability to pay extravagant compliments on behalf of the university. It so happened that the first letter which he wrote as Orator was addressed to no less a person than King James himself, thanking him for his gift to Cambridge of his *Opera Latina*. Herbert, who had already in his lectures publicly demonstrated his admiration for the king's latinity, must have undertaken this task with alacrity. He appended to the letter an epigram of fulsome flattery, which may well have succeeded in its purpose of catching the fancy of the king.

According to Walton, James came often to hunt at Newmarket and Royston, and he formed a most favourable impression of the courtier-like young don who used to welcome him to Cambridge "with *Gratulations* and the *Applauses* of an Orator". George Herbert had, besides, a very powerful friend at court. His kinsman, William, Earl of Pembroke, was at that time Lord Chamberlain to the King, and Walton relates how he spoke up in favour of his cousin, saying that "he lov'd him more for his learning and verture, than for that he was of his name and family. At which answer the King smil'd, and asked the Earl leave, that he might love him too; for he took him to be the Jewel of that University" (p. 271).

This Earl of Pembroke and his brother Philip, who succeeded to the title, were sons of the famous Lady Mary Herbert, sister of Sir Philip Sidney; and it was to this "Most Noble and Incomparable Pair of Brethren" that Heminge and Condell dedicated the First Folio of Shakespeare's Works in 1623. Aubrey, who was a Wiltshire man and knew Wilton well, speaks of William, Earl of Pembroke, as "a most noble Person, and the Glory of the Court in the Reignes of King James and King Charles. He was handsome and of an

The Layman

admirable presence. He was the greatest Maecenas to learned Men of any Peer of his time: or since ... He was of an Heroiq, and publick Spirit, Bountiful to his Friends, and Servants, and a great Encourager of Learned Men".[1] Lord Pembroke may well have been speaking the truth when he declared to the king that he esteemed his young kinsman George Herbert more for his gifts than on the score of their family connection.

But the powerful Lord Pembroke and his brother were not the only Herberts with whom King James was acquainted. George's eldest brother, Edward, later created Baron Herbert of Cherbury, had made his mark as a courtier and was at this very time Ambassador in Paris; and in 1621 Henry, George's younger and favourite brother, on returning from his studies in France, became a gentleman of the King's privy chamber, and was appointed Master of the Revels in 1623.

We have little positive evidence of what George Herbert was doing between 1621 and 1625, but he appears to have written no letters on behalf of the university after October 1621; and though he delivered three orations in 1623, he was almost certainly, as Walton alleges, often away from Cambridge, being more taken up with the court and with his chances of promotion through the king's favour than with the claims of the university. His predecessor in the Oratorship, Sir Francis Nethersole, had become a Secretary of State upon giving up office at Cambridge, and Walton suggests that Herbert applied himself to the study of Italian, Spanish and French "at this time of being Orator ... hoping, that as his Predecessors, so he might in time attain the place of a *Secretary of State*, he being at that time very high in the King's favour; and not meanly valued and lov'd by the most eminent and most powerful of the Court-Nobility" (p. 274).

Walton also says that the King gave Herbert a sinecure

[1] *op. cit.* p. 145.

George Herbert

worth a hundred and twenty pounds a year. Later biographers have not been able to establish what this sinecure was; but there is no reason to doubt that King James did reward the young Orator with an allowance, so that "with his Annuity, and the advantage of his Colledge, and of his Oratorship, he enjoyed his gentile humor for cloaths, and Court-like company, and seldom look'd towards *Cambridge*, unless the King were there, but then he never fail'd..." (p. 275).

The Court was not merely a spring-board for men ambitious of public office; it was the focus of all talent, literary and artistic, and its patronage extended to preachers and divines as well as to playwrights and poets. Lancelot Andrewes and John Donne owed a good deal to the favours of King James, who in spite of his drunkenness was seriously interested in theology. George Herbert, in attaching himself to the Court, was doing neither more nor less than a gentleman in his circumstances might be expected to do. Even his mother, anxious that he should take holy orders, may well have imagined that the King would give him some important church preferment. Advancement, however, did not come his way. Walton suggests that when the King died, in 1625, shortly after the decease of two of Herbert's most influential patrons, the Duke of Richmond and the Marquis of Hamilton, "all Mr. *Herbert's* Court-hopes" died with them. Other factors, however, must have been at work to destroy them. Had Herbert wished, he could undoubtedly have won the favour of King Charles, whose court was notably more sober, more cultivated and better conducted than that of his father. Even the puritanical Mrs. Lucy Hutchinson admitted that "The face of the Court was much changed in the change of the King, for King Charles was temperate, chaste and serious ... Men of learning and ingenuity in all the arts were in esteem, and received encouragement of the king, who was a most excellent judge and a great lover of paintings, carvings,

The Layman

gravings, and many other ingenuities, less offensive than the bawdry and profane abusive wit of the other Court."[1]

Possibly it was the dissoluteness of James' court that determined George Herbert to think again before soliciting the favour of the new king and continuing his rather unprofitable mode of life. Possibly the abrupt recall of his brother Edward from the Ambassadorship in Paris had something to do with it; for though he was given an Irish barony, the Stuarts never quite forgave him for his plain speaking on the marriage of the Prince of Wales to Henrietta Maria. Sir Henry Herbert, however, remained attached to the Court after the death of King James, and if George had elected to stay there, he would surely have been welcome.

The strange thing is that Herbert, having received a good many marks of favour from James, should not have pronounced the commemorative oration at Cambridge after the king's death. He left this task to the deputy Orator, his friend Thorndyke. Nor did he contribute any Latin poem to the collection of elegies made in memory of the king. This omission is the more remarkable since he went out of his way in the following year to contribute, in his capacity as Public Orator, some Latin verses to a commemorative volume in honour of Bacon, with whom he had been on friendly terms for some years.

Since the Lord Chancellor died in disgrace, he did not receive from the university of Cambridge the official tribute that would have been his due; but a volume of elegies was published in London in 1626. The only other university dignitary besides Herbert who contributed verses was the Provost of King's; but the book contained elegies by several Westminster and Trinity men, who may have been encouraged by Herbert to pay their last respects to a great

[1] *Memoirs of the Life of Colonel Hutchinson,* ed. C. H. Firth, Routledge, 1906, p. 64.

George Herbert

Englishman. In the year of his death, Bacon had dedicated his "translation of Certaine Psalms into English Verse" to "his very good friend Mr. George Herbert", alluding in the dedication to Herbert's share in translating *The Advancement of Learning* into Latin and remarking on his poetic judgment. But if Herbert owed a courtesy to Bacon, so he did to King James, and it is puzzling that he should have omitted to pay it.

At the time of the king's death George Herbert was thirty-two; and the loss of three of his patrons so shook him that he went for a while to stay quietly in the country (we do not know where) in order to take stock of himself and his prospects. His life up to that point had been agreeable and interesting, if not outstandingly successful. At his mother's house, at Cambridge, at Court, he had moved as an equal among distinguished people. There had never been anything narrow in his environment, nor was he at any time censorious in his attitude to "the world", or to those who differed from him in religious conviction.

When Edward Herbert made a draft of *De Veritate* in 1622, he dedicated it to his brother George and to William Boswell, his secretary in Paris, on the understanding that they should expunge anything which they found in it contrary to good morals or the true Catholic faith. The central thesis of the book is that the beliefs essential to salvation commend themselves to the reason and are to be found incorporated in all religions. That George Herbert did not censor the draft testifies to his fair-mindedness and powers of discrimination. Though he himself abhorred speculation, he was prepared to let others speculate and even question the fundamentals of the Christian faith.

Nor is there anything in his poetry that parallels Spenser's *Colin Clout's Come Home Again:* no poem of bitter disillusion with the vanities of the scheming world, no denunciation of

The Layman

the hollow shams of Court life. In *The Pearl* Herbert tells how he knows the ways of Learning, the ways of Honour, and the ways of Pleasure, and he underrates none of them. He was too honest to deny, at any stage of his life, that he found great satisfaction in exercising his gifts in secular employments. This humane acceptance of the world as he found it saved him from any excess of remorse for wasted time and from puritanical condemnation of the kind of life that ultimately he abandoned. It also made the renunciation of this worldly life a costly sacrifice. Learning, Honour, Pleasure—

> I know all these, and have them in my hand:
> Therefore not sealed, but with open eyes
> I flie to thee, and fully understand
> Both the main sale, and the commodities;
> And at what rate and price I have thy love;
> With all the circumstances that may move.
> *(The Pearl, p. 89.)*

Ever since childhood, George Herbert had been aware of the claims which the love of God made upon him, and the time had come when he could no longer set them aside. Towards the end of 1625, returning to London from his sojourn in the country—Walton mentions an unidentified friend in Kent with whom he stayed—he announced his resolution to enter into holy orders.

Whether George Herbert had already made up his mind to this course before he went to London we do not know; but if he was still irresolute he must have been powerfully swayed by finding John Donne a fellow-guest in the home of his mother and Sir John Danvers. Donne, by this time Dean of St. Paul's and the most famous preacher in England, had gone to Chelsea, then a village, to escape the plague that was ravaging the city of London. Danvers' house, built on the site of the country house of Sir Thomas More and

George Herbert

surrounded by the celebrated Italian gardens, was a retreat to which many distinguished people came with pleasure.

Strong influences combined to work upon George Herbert at this juncture, confirming him in his decision, if he had already reached it, impelling him towards it, if he had not. There was the threat of the plague, raging a few miles away, forcing upon him the stark need for redeeming the time. There was the presence of Dr. Donne, his mother's old friend, who had himself renounced the world, the flesh and the devil in order to dedicate himself, as a priest, to the service of God. There was his mother herself, now in failing health and visited by attacks of melancholy. She had always believed him to be destined for the priesthood, and at this crisis in his life she must have encouraged him with all her heart to seek ordination. Nor can we doubt that George Herbert discussed with Donne the conflict that he had taken so long to resolve; for who better could understand the difficulties besetting a man drawn to God's service yet hesitating to surrender? At all events, by the end of 1625, Herbert had made up his mind to take holy orders, and in the following year he was ordained deacon.

This did not involve him in the work of a parish. In July 1626 he was instituted by proxy at Lincoln Cathedral to the canonry and prebend of Leighton Ecclesia, a sinecure that carried with it only the duty of preaching once a year in the cathedral; and even that could be done by a deputy. The parish, now known as Leighton Bromswold, had its own vicar, and though later Herbert was to take an active interest in the rebuilding of the church, there is no record that he ever officiated there, or indeed ever visited it. He held another small sinecure in Montgomeryshire.

Although in deacon's orders, Herbert continued to dress as a layman, still wearing a sword, and he led a layman's life, if a very retired and sober one. He did not give up his

The Layman

Oratorship till 1627, a few months after the death of his mother. According to Walton, it was only to please her that he kept it on so long. He appears to have delivered an oration in July 1626, when the Duke of Buckingham was installed as Chancellor of Cambridge; and in the same year, as has already been mentioned, he had a good deal to do with the publication of a volume of commemorative verse in honour of Lord Chancellor Bacon.

Herbert's health, never robust, seems at this period of his life to have been particularly poor. The damp climate of Cambridge had never suited him, as it fostered his tendency to ague "and other infirmities which he judg'd were increasd by his studies". In his thirty-fourth year he was seized, according to Walton, "with a sharp *Quotidian Ague*, and thought to remove it by the change of Air" (p. 284). Accordingly he went to stay for some months with his brother Henry, who was living at Woodford in Essex. Here, by strict attention to diet, he managed to rid himself of the ague, but not of a susceptibility to "Rheums and other weaknesses, and a supposed consumption".

He was not the only member of his family to suffer from these tendencies. His eldest sister, Elizabeth, "my dear sick sister" as he calls her in several letters, lived for many years with her mother in London, although her husband and children were in Wales, in order to have better medical care in her consumptive state. Edward Herbert in his *Autobiography* says that: "For the space of about fourteen years, she languished and pined away to skin and bones."[1] However, she outlived her brother George by about a year. He wrote to her, and of her, in the most affectionate terms; but indeed, he seems to have been a very good brother. He travelled up to Lincoln to see his sister Frances just when he was getting embroiled in the contention for the Public Oratorship; and

[1] *op. cit.* p. 14.

after the death of his sister Margaret, when he himself was married and established at Bemerton, he took all her three daughters into his household. His brothers Edward and Henry both professed interest in the orphans, and were better able to afford the expense of caring for them than George was; but he, for the sake of the girls themselves, preferred not to separate them, though the three must have been something of a burden.

Nothing is known of his relations with his brother Charles, the other scholarly member of the family, who was a Fellow of New College, Oxford. As he died at the age of twenty five, we may imagine that he too was constitutionally delicate.

Of his relations with the most interesting of his brothers, Edward, Lord Herbert of Cherbury, we know tantalisingly little. In the *Autobiography*, written some years after George's death, Edward refers to him in terms of great esteem. Some of his English works, he says, "are extant, which, though they be rare in their kind, yet are far short of those perfections he had in the Greek and Latin tongues, and all divine and human literature". An interesting comment refers to his quick temper. "He was not exempt from passion and choler, being infirmities to which all our race is subject, but that excepted, without reproach in his actions".[1] Allusion is also made to the reputation for saintliness which he acquired in the neighbourhood of Salisbury when he was beneficed there; though his brother, in speaking of the "many years" he spent in his country parish, had evidently forgotten the shortness of his actual ministry at Bemerton, less than three years.

Edward Herbert's mind was so markedly original, and his researches into the nature of truth so unorthodox, that his great regard for George is the more striking. Proof of his respect for his judgment has already been given. One would give much to have George's comments on the draft of

[1] *op. cit.* p. 11.

The Layman

De Veritate and on such poems of Edward's as he may have seen. Skill in versifying, a passionate love of music, and an interest in botany were common to both brothers; but their temperaments were diametrically opposed. Edward Herbert, dashing, quarrelsome, intensely conceited and outrageously boastful, scarcely speaks in his autobiography of his serious pursuits. Though he was a philosopher of real originality, and a metaphysical poet of great talent, he refers to his writings as though they were the merest by-products of his leisure. This was a typically renaissance affectation, a display of *sprezzatura* by a soldierly, courtly man of the world. He spent so much of his earlier life abroad that there were not, in fact, many opportunities for him and his brother George to become intimate. There was ten years difference in age between them; and if, as seems likely, Edward resented his young step-father, he may have spent little time under his mother's roof.

With Henry, younger than himself, George seems always to have been on particularly friendly terms; and his sojourn at Woodford in 1626 apparently lasted for the best part of a year. In the following year his mother died; and this bereft him of a strong supporting influence and deepened the dejection from which he was suffering at this period. Ill-health may have been the main reason for his failure to seek ordination as a priest after the usual interval of one year after taking deacon's orders; but if, as seems certain, many of his poems were written at this time, he was suffering too from indecision, discontent and a sense of uselessness. His mother's death was another blow.

He wrote a series of poems, *Memoriae Matris Sacrum*, fourteen of which are in Latin and five in Greek, and these were printed together with Donne's funeral sermon. He may have chosen the learned languages in a desire to do his mother greater honour, feeling that they were better suited than

George Herbert

English to the solemnity of elegy. It is impossible not to regret that he did not, on this occasion, permit himself to write, in English, poetry springing from the love of a human creature. Nevertheless, the memorial poems, besides painting a most attractive portrait of Mrs. Herbert, show clearly enough his strong sense of dependence on his mother:

> Per te nascor in hunc globum
> Exemplóque tuo nascor in alterum:
>   Bis tu mater eras mihi . . . (p. 425)

In another poem, englished by Mr. Blunden, he declares:

> Thou wast my root, my solid rock, and I
> A *Polypus*, held tight and safe thereby;
> Not only the Dark Sisters cut thy thread;
> Their shears touched me, and I with thee seem dead.[1]

Little is known of George Herbert's movements during the year of his mother's death; but in 1628, seeking another change of air, he went to Wiltshire, to stay with his stepfather's eldest brother, the Earl of Danby; and with this visit to Wiltshire another chapter in his life began.

---

[1] Edmund Blunden, *George Herbert's Latin Poems,* Essays & Studies of the English Association, xix, 1934. Latin original on p. 428 of *Works.*

II

The Priest

THE seat of the Earl of Danby was Dauntsey House, near Chippenham; and there George Herbert was, according to Walton, given an apartment such "as might best sute with his accomodation and liking. And in this place, by a *spare Dyet,* declining all *perplexing Studies,* by *moderate exercise,* and a *chearful conversation,* his health was apparently improv'd to a good degree of health and chearfulness; And then, he declar'd his resolution both to marry, and to enter into the Sacred Orders of Priesthood" (p. 285).

If Herbert had ever at an earlier stage contemplated marriage, there is no record or even rumour of it. As long as he held a College Fellowship he was, of course, pledged to celibacy, and at Court he seems to have lived in an exemplary manner; but he was an emotional, highly sensitive man, and if he led an ascetic life it was not because he was naturally cold or rigid.

> I know the ways of Pleasure, the sweet strains,
> The lullings and the relishes of it;
> The propositions of hot bloud and brains;
> What mirth and musick mean; what love and wit
> Have done these twentie hundred yeares, and more:
> I know the projects of unbridled store:
> My stuffe is flesh, not brasse; my senses live,
> And grumble oft, that they have more in me
> Then he that curbs them, being but one to five.
> *(The Pearl,* p. 89.)

George Herbert

Walton gives an engaging but apocryphal account of how George Herbert and Jane Danvers fell in love by hearsay. His whole picture of their relationship is painted in the rosiest tones; but when one remembers how caustically he dealt with Hooker's marriage, there is good reason for supposing that he was not falsifying his effects. Certainly Herbert chose a wife well suited to him as far as worldly considerations go. Jane Danvers was a cousin of his own step-father, and was living with her widowed mother at Baynton House in the parish of Edington, not far from Lord Danby's estate. The Danvers had been a prominent Wiltshire family before the time when William Herbert, the first Earl of Pembroke, came from the Welsh marches to establish himself at Wilton as one of the great landowners of the county. Jane Danvers was a well-bred young woman with money of her own. Aubrey, who had a Danvers grandmother, observes: "My kinswoman was a handsome *bona roba*, and ingeniose."[1] She was certainly not at all the typical parson's wife of the period, any more than George Herbert was the typical parson.

Their marriage took place at Edington Church on 5th March 1628/9. According to Aubrey, Herbert "when he was married lived a yeare or better at Dauntsey House"; but according to Walton, they were at Baynton when Arthur Woodnoth (his informant) visited them a year after their wedding. At all events, they remained in Wiltshire; and it was in this county that Herbert was to spend the rest of his life.

At the time of their marriage he was, though in deacon's orders, still living as a private gentleman, and had not "chang'd his sword and silk Cloaths into a Canonical Coat" (p. 291). This was against the rubric, but Herbert was notoriously over-concerned about his clothes. Walton reports that at Cambridge "If during this time he exprest any Error, it was that he

[1] *op. cit.* p. 137.

The Priest

kept himself too much retir'd, and at too great distance with all his inferiours; and his cloaths seem'd to prove, that he put too great a value on his parts and Parentage" (p. 270).

His wife, according to Walton, did not at all demur at her change of status when he became a priest. He lost no time in admonishing her that she must now so far forget her father's house as not to claim a precedence over any of her parishioners, and to this she cheerfully agreed. Her natural and happy humility "begot her an unfeigned love, and a serviceable respect from all that convers't with her; and this love followed her in all places, as inseparably, as shadows follow substances in Sunshine" (p. 291).

There was such perfect affection between George Herbert and his wife, says Walton, that "there was never any opposition betwixt them, unless it were a Contest which should most incline to a compliance with the others desires" (p. 286). She acted as her husband's almoner, ordered his household, and supported him in all his endeavours. So we are told by Walton. George Herbert himself is entirely silent on the subject of his marriage. He mentions Jane in his will as "my deare Wife", and bequeaths her the bulk of his property; but otherwise he does not directly refer to her, except to add her greetings when he writes letters to his friends. It was against Herbert's principles to address love-poems to any other recipient than his God; and we cannot infer that the wife in *The Country Parson* is a delineation of his own wife. There is no reason to doubt, however, that Jane Danvers was as good a helpmeet to her husband as the hypothetical lady in the book, nor that she possessed a greater share of "beauty, riches and honour ... the qualities of the world" than Herbert advised his ideal parson to look for when choosing a partner.

Though from boyhood George Herbert had considered dedicating his life as well as his art to God's service, the actual taking of priest's orders was a step which he dreaded.

George Herbert

Ambition and an attachment to the world were the main factors that held him back for years from being ordained a deacon. Having reached this stage, which meant the abandonment of all hopes of a career in the service of the state, he was held back from the priesthood by considerations of a very different kind. Doubts of his own worthiness now beset him.

> Blest Order, which in power dost so excell,
> That with th' one hand thou liftest to the sky,
> And with the other throwest down to hell
> In thy just censures; fain would I draw nigh,
> Fain put thee on, exchanging my lay-sword
>   For that of th' Holy Word.
>
> But thou art fire, sacred and hallow'd fire;
> And I but earth and clay: should I presume
> To wear thy habit, the severe attire
> My slender compositions might consume.
> I am both foul and brittle; much unfit
>   To deal in holy Writ.
>
> *(The Priesthood,* p. 160.)

Herbert's regard for the priestly office was grounded in his profound reverence for the holy mysteries which all priests are called upon to celebrate and expound:

> But th' holy men of God such vessels are,
> As serve him up, who all the world commands:
> When God vouchsafeth to become our fare,
> Their hands convey him, who conveys their hands.
>
> *(ibid,* p. 161.)

Thoughts such as these made Herbert "fast and pray often, and consider for not less than a month" (p. 287) when the Earl of Pembroke, early in 1630, offered him a neglected little

The Priest

parish lying between Wilton and Salisbury. It was doubtless a wish to have George Herbert as domestic chaplain at Wilton, rather than any concern for the welfare of the three hundred parishioners of Fugglestone St. Peter and Bemerton St. Andrew, that induced Lord Pembroke to propose him for the benefice; but Herbert was deeply perturbed by "the apprehension of the last great Account that he was to make for the Cure of so many souls", and after a month's delay he had not made up his mind to accept the presentation.

The previous holder of the living, Dr. Curll, had not resided there; he resigned the benefice on being appointed Bishop of Bath and Wells. Though Lord Pembroke was normally patron of the living, King Charles on this occasion had to make the presentation, since he had promoted the outgoing rector. According to Walton, Pembroke "requested the King to bestow it upon his kinsman, *George Herbert*; and the King said, *Most willingly to* Mr. Herbert, *if it be worth his acceptance*" (p. 287).

He might well have wondered whether so scholarly and courtly a gentleman, with a newly married wife from one of the great Wiltshire families, would be attracted by such an offer. It was most unusual at this period for anyone of Herbert's birth and education to become a mere country parson. To take orders at all was an unusual step for a man of breeding. Donne, in his verse-letter *To Mr. Tilman after he had taken orders* mentions "Lay-scornings of the Ministry" and asks

> Why doth the foolish world scorne that profession
> Whose joyes passe speech? Why do they think unfit
> That Gentry should joyne families with it?[1]

Herbert himself speaks of "the generall ignominy cast upon the profession" of a country parson, and Barnabas Oley, the

---
[1] *The Divine Poems,* ed. H. Gardner, Oxford, 1952, p. 32.

first editor of *A Priest to the Temple*, remarks that he had heard men censure Herbert "as a man that did not manage his brave parts to his best advantage, but lost himself in an humble way."[1]

Besides these considerations, there was the fact that the parish offered was a small and neglected one. The two churches were in need of repair; the one at Bemerton, a stone's throw from the rectory, was described justly enough by Aubrey as a pitiful little chapel of ease. The rectory itself was unfit to live in, since it had not been recently inhabited. The one attraction of the place was the nearness of Wilton House; but if Lord Pembroke or the King imagined that Herbert was going to spend most of his time there, they were mistaken.

Wilton House was then, as it had been in the days of "Sidney's sister, Pembroke's mother", a centre of culture and elegance, a stately house which monarchs and their courts were wont to visit. It does not, however, appear that the Court was either at Wilton or at Salisbury in the spring of 1630. Consequently Walton's story is more charming than true, of how George Herbert, accompanied by his friend Arthur Woodnoth, went to Wilton to explain his hesitation about accepting the offer of Bemerton, and was only persuaded to take it by the united efforts of the King, Laud and Pembroke. Apocryphal, too, is the pleasant anecdote of the tailor, who "was sent for to come speedily from *Salisbury* to *Wilton*, to take measure, and make him some Canonical Cloaths, against next day; which the Taylor did; and Mr. *Herbert* being so habited, went with his presentation to the learned Dr. Davenant, who was then Bishop of Salisbury" (p. 288), to be instituted and inducted on that very same day into the living of Bemerton.

Actually the deed of presentation of the rectory to Herbert

[1] *A Priest to the Temple*, 2nd ed., 1671, M. 3.

The Priest

is dated from Westminster, 16th of April, 1630. Ten days later he was instituted at Salisbury by Dr. Davenant, and on the same day (which is the date given by Walton) he was inducted at Bemerton Church. Not until September 19th was he ordained priest by the Bishop of Salisbury in the Cathedral. His priesthood lasted only two and a half years, his incumbency of Bemerton less than three.

Walton's story of the day of his induction derives from Arthur Woodnoth, who was a cousin of the Ferrars of Little Gidding and a reliable witness. "When at his Induction he was shut into *Bemerton* Church, being left alone there to Toll the Bell (as the Law requires him): he staid so much longer than an ordinary time, before he return'd to those Friends that staid expecting him at the Church-door, that his friend, Mr. *Woodnot*, look'd in at the Church-window, and saw him lie prostrate on the ground before the Altar: at which time and place (as he after told Mr. *Woodnot*) he set some Rules to himself, for the future manage of his life; and then and there made a vow, to labour to keep them" (p. 289).

Herbert, lying in abasement and self-consecration before the altar, had reached the crux of his life. His surrender had been long delayed, but it was absolute and transforming. Men do not achieve saintliness by an iron determination to lead a devout life according to rule. This conscious striving after virtue will change their habits, but not necessarily their hearts. Grace is needed for that; and grace was certainly granted to George Herbert. Real holiness of character differs from moral righteousness in being immediately attractive to all kinds of people; and what evidence we have goes to show that Herbert, as a priest in his little rural parish, was beloved and revered by all who knew him, because of his unmistakable goodness. Walton has been blamed for beatifying him too easily and enthusiastically, but Ferrar

George Herbert

and Oley and Edward Herbert are earlier witnesses to his reputation for sanctity; and we are constantly struck by the beauty of character that his writings reveal.

This beauty, naturally, was the fruit of his whole life, not the result of a sudden conversion. It may indeed be doubted whether Herbert was a "twice-born" man. The effect of his decision was to strengthen and stabilize the relationship between himself and his divine Master of which he had been conscious since boyhood.

> When first thy sweet and gracious eye
> Vouchsaf'd even in the midst of youth and night
> To look upon me, who before did lie
>   Weltring in sinne;
> I felt a sugred strange delight,
> Passing all cordials made by any art,
> Bedew, embalme, and overrunne my heart,
>   And take it inne.
>
> Since that time many a bitter storm
> My soul hath felt, ev'n able to destroy,
> Had the malicious and ill-meaning harm
>   His swing and sway:
> But still thy sweet originall joy,
> Sprung from thine eye, did work within my soul,
> And surging griefs, when they grew bold, controll,
>   And got the day.
>   (*The Glance*, p. 171.)

There is much in Walton's life to suggest that George Herbert's was *anima naturaliter christiana*. Certainly the most characteristic notes in his poetry are the authentically Christian ones—notes that Milton too rarely sounds—of humility, compassion and responsiveness to the love of God. Yet the record of his life before he became a priest shows that he had his full share of pride, ambition and self-will.

The Priest

The conflict between the claims of religion and worldliness was long and intense; and it is the sensitiveness of the conscience that eventually decides the magnitude of any offence, not the verdict of outside observers. Donne may seem to us to have had more to repent of than Herbert; but we are, in fact, quite incompetent to judge.

It does appear, however, that Herbert escaped one affliction that usually assails religiously-minded people. Intellectually, he assented to the whole Christian faith as taught by his Mother Church, and showed no wish to rebel against its tenets. Donne was never at ease in the church of his adoption, nor would he have been satisfied if he had remained a Roman Catholic. He was by nature a sceptic, or at most a moral individualist, whereas Herbert was a natural believer. It was not Herbert's mind that rebelled against the vocation of priesthood; it was, as he himself recognized and acknowledged with perfect clearness, his will. Even when at last he subjected this stubborn will to the will of God, he did not find lasting serenity. His emotional dependence on his divine Master became greater than before, and he was the more acutely conscious of alienation, when it came; but he did, by the surrender of his self-will, achieve a wonderful singleness of purpose.

He could not at once settle down to his parochial duties, for the rectory needed extensive rebuilding, and both churches had to be repaired. His wife appears to have stayed at Baynton with her mother while these alterations were carried out, and Walton suggests that Herbert, too, made it his headquarters, though he was often in his parish, supervising the building and making the acquaintance of his people. Within a few months, the Herberts established themselves in a comfortable though quite unpretentious house—smaller than the present Bemerton Rectory, which was enlarged by a Victorian incumbent. Across the road from their front door, over-

George Herbert

looked by the windows of Herbert's study, lay the tiny church of St. Andrew; behind the house the garden sloped down to the river Nadder. "Mr. Herbert made a good garden and walks" reports Aubrey;[1] and a mulberry tree still growing there is ascribed to his planting. In *The Country Parson* Herbert displays a familiar knowledge of the use of herbs and simples: "esteeming that there is no spice comparable, for herbs, to rosemary, time, savoury, mints; and for seeds, to Fennell, and Carroway seeds. Accordingly, for salves, his wife seeks not the city, but prefers her garden and fields before all outlandish gums. And surely hyssope, valerian, mercury, adders tongue, yerrow, melilot, and Saint *Johns* wort made into a salve; and Elder, camomill, mallowes, comphrey and smallage made into a Poultis, have done great and rare cures" (p. 262).

The Herberts had no children of their own; but they had not been long settled at Bemerton before two orphaned nieces joined them, and later a third. Four maidservants and two men are mentioned in Herbert's will, and he also maintained a curate, Nathaniel Bostock; towards the end of his life he was obliged to employ a second curate. His expenses, therefore, were considerable, and it is not surprising that, writing to his brother Henry, he should describe himself as "more beggarly now than I have been these many years ... but difficulties are so farr from cooling christians, that they whett them" (p. 376).

A proof of this last assertion may be found in George Herbert's activity, during his years at Bemerton, in raising funds for the restoration of the church of Leighton Bromswold, in Huntingdonshire. He had held the prebend of this parish since his ordination in 1626, and at one time—presumably troubled because he was contributing nothing towards the welfare of the place—he had done his best to persuade his

[1] *op. cit.* p. 137.

The Priest

friend Nicholas Ferrar, who was also in deacon's orders, to accept it. Ferrar's home at Little Gidding lay only a few miles from Leighton; but he put forward the alternative proposal, that Herbert should rather take an active interest in Leighton and collect money towards the "reedifying of the Church belonging thereunto, that had layen ruinated almost twenty years",[1] the vicar being obliged to hold the services in the great hall of the Duke of Lenox's mansion.

Several letters from Herbert on this topic are extant, and they show the enthusiasm with which he set about collecting funds, enlisting the help of his brother Henry. He also took a practical interest in the actual work of rebuilding, which was supervised by Nicholas Ferrar and his brother John, the accounts of the building fund being kept by Arthur Woodnoth. Herbert left £15 in his will towards the rebuilding of Leighton church, but he had the satisfaction before he died of knowing that sufficient money had already been contributed to ensure its being put into good order. The woodwork of the church, and the identical pulpit and reading desk on either side of the chancel, remain to this day as they were installed; and the tower of the church was built as a memorial to George Herbert, soon after his death, by the fourth Duke of Lenox.

The friendship between Herbert and Nicholas Ferrar was very warm and deep. When writing to him, Herbert addressed him as "My exceeding dear Brother", and it was to him that he entrusted the manuscript of his poems when he knew that he was dying. There is, however, no record of their meeting, and Barnabas Oley as well as Walton remarks that their friendship was maintained entirely by the exchange of letters.

"There is another thing," says Oley, "(some will call it a Paradox) which I learned from Him (and Mr. Ferrar) in the

[1] Preface to *The Temple*. *Works*, p. 4.

George Herbert

Managery of their most cordial and *Christian Friendship.* That this may be maintained in vigour and height without the Ceremonies of Visits and Complements; yea, without any Trade of secular courtesies, meerly in order to spiritual Edification of one another in love. I know they loved each other most entirely, and their very souls cleaved together most intimately, and drove a large flock of Christian intelligence together long before their deaths; yet saw they not each other in many years; I think scarce ever, but as Members of one University, in their whole lives."[1] Walton notes that, being contemporaries at Cambridge, they had begun a slight acquaintanceship there, which was renewed in after life when both were endeavouring to establish a pattern of devout Anglican living: "and this new holy friendship was long maintain'd without any interview, but only by loving and endearing letters" (p. 312).

Only three letters from Herbert to Ferrar have survived, and two of them deal with the rebuilding of Leighton. It is hard to credit that Herbert should never have visited this prebend of his, or his friend's famous establishment at Little Gidding. Near to one another, they are both within easy reach of Cambridge; and he did not sever his connection with the university until he had already been in deacon's orders for about a year. There was undoubtedly a good deal of intercourse between Little Gidding and Bemerton, for we know of visits by Woodnoth and Duncon, both associates of Ferrar. Books, too, were exchanged. Herbert probably owned one of the famous Little Gidding Concordances, with illustrations taken from foreign Emblem Books; and one of the Little Gidding Story Books contains more than two hundred proverbs that correspond with proverbs in the collection that George Herbert is supposed to have compiled. His brief notes on Valdesso's *Considerations* were undertaken at the

[1] *op. cit.* N6.

The Priest

express desire of Nicholas Ferrar, who had translated the work from an Italian version of the Spanish original; and it is likely that Herbert sent a manuscript copy of his own translation of Cornaro's *Treatise on Temperance and Sobriety* to the Ferrars, who were interested in questions of health and diet.

Nicholas Ferrar's brief preface to *The Temple* is the earliest written record of George Herbert's life. He spoke with authority about his priesthood, "wherein his faithfull discharge was such, as may make him justly a companion to the primitive Saints, and a pattern or more for the age he lived in" (p. 3). These words were written within a year of Herbert's death; they deal with fact, not with pious legend. "His obedience and conformitie to the Church and the discipline thereof was singularly remarkable. Though he abounded in private devotions, yet went he every morning and evening with his familie to the Church: and by his example, exhortations and encouragements drew the greater part of his parishioners to accompanie him dayly in the publick celebration of Divine Service" (p. 4).

The best testimony to Herbert's holiness of life as a parish priest is his own book, *A Priest to the Temple,* written at Bemerton. He wrote it that he might have, in his own words, "a mark to aim at"; but only a man who had already achieved a measure of saintliness could have set down his ideals with such shining and single-hearted devotion. The true priest, as Herbert pictures him, is no scholarly contemplative, but a man who, like his Master, goes about doing good: "Love is his businesse and aim." In church, his care is to glorify God by a form of worship that is perfectly intelligible to all those taking part in it. To this end, his sermons are simply-worded explanations, his catechizing constant and searching. Barnabas Oley remarks in his preface to *A Priest to the Temple* that "The chief aim of Master F(errar) and this Author, was to win those that dislike our

George Herbert

Liturgy, Catechism, etc. by the constant, Reverent and Holy use of them."[1] In the parish, Herbert made it his business to care for the physical as well as the spiritual well-being of his people. If he fulfilled even half the programme he proposed to himself in his pastoral treatise, his time was well spent. Not for nothing was he the son of Magdalen Herbert and the grandson of Magdalen Newport, whose practical charity was as outstanding as their piety.

The treatise must not be read as though it were autobiographical. Herbert explains in the preface that he was setting down his ideals, and that they were high ones, well beyond his reach; but "it is a good strife to go as farre as wee can in pleasing of him, who hath done so much for us" (p. 226). In spite of this, the book is indirectly, perhaps unconsciously, self-revealing. Its blend of shrewdness with spiritual wisdom is thoroughly characteristic of Herbert.

Though his life had been wholly spent among sophisticated people, he writes of country folk as though he had been brought up among them, with a sympathetic understanding of their needs as well as a humorous eye for their shortcomings. Sometimes his old fastidiousness creeps in, as when he speaks of the parson's apparel being "plaine, but reverend and clean, without spots, or dust, or smell; the purity of his mind breaking out, and dilating it selfe even to his body, cloaths and habitation" (p. 228). Or again, when he observes that the parson must not disdain to "enter into the poorest Cottage, though he even creep into it, and though it smell never so lothsomly. For both God is there, and those for whom God dyed" (p. 249). The complete sincerity of Herbert's Christianity comes out beautifully in this last sentence, and in the way in which it qualifies the foregoing one.

Sometimes he lets fall observations that have a personal

[1] *op. cit.* M5.

The Priest

ring, as when he remarks that "Ambition, or an untimely desire of promotion to an higher state, or place, under colour of accommodation, or necessary provision, is a common temptation to men of any eminency, especially being single men" (p. 238). He goes on immediately to say that "Curiosity in prying into high speculative and unprofitable questions is another great stumbling block to the holinesse of Scholars"; but if this was one of his own temptations, he seems to have been successful in vanquishing it. The courtesy which he recommends to his ideal country parson is a quality that reveals itself again and again in the book, in his imaginative consideration for the feelings of others. When he treats of reproofs, he urges the necessity for gentleness and careful timing, and when he recommends hospitality, he explains that all, irrespective of their rank, must be equally welcome to the parson's table.

His early biographers make it clear that the conduct of daily public worship in the church, and his own private devotions, were the activities to which Herbert attached supreme importance. How much of the parish work he assigned to Nathaniel Bostock we have no means of knowing; but priestly and pastoral duties made their double claim on his time and strength.

He seems, besides, to have acted as chaplain at Wilton, a task that must have called for all his tact. After the death, just before Herbert's induction to Bemerton, of William Earl of Pembroke, his brother Philip, succeeding to the title, married Lady Anne Clifford, widow of the Earl of Dorset, and proceeded to neglect and ill-treat her. She was a gifted and well-read woman, and that Herbert was on good terms with her is shown by a sympathetic letter in which he sent her "a Priest's blessing" while she was at Court.

Herbert's various activities included the writing of his pastoral treatise and some translations undertaken for Nicholas

George Herbert

Ferrar; but of all his work at Bemerton the activity that most concerns us today is his writing of poetry. More than half the poems contained in *The Temple* were written during Herbert's priesthood, and the others were revised. We know that he took great pains in fashioning and polishing his verse, and he seems to have circulated some of it in manuscript, for he had a certain reputation as a poet before his death, though none of his English poems were in print. What value did George Herbert attach to his poetry? And what importance did the writing of it actually have in his life?

The first question is comparatively easy to answer, for we have the story of the bequest of the manuscript of *The Temple* to Nicholas Ferrar, recounted to Walton by Edmond Duncon himself, the man who conveyed the book and Herbert's message to Little Gidding. The words attributed to Herbert have the ring of truth. "Sir, I pray deliver this little Book to my dear brother *Farrer,* and tell him, he shall find in it a picture of the many spiritual Conflicts that have past betwixt God and my Soul, before I could subject mine to the will of *Jesus my Master*: in whose service I have now found perfect freedom; desire him to read it: and then, if he can think it may turn to the advantage of any dejected poor Soul, let it be made publick; if not, let him burn it: for I and it, are less than the least of God's mercies" (p. 314).

Herbert's humility is touching; but the very fact that he so carefully entrusted the book to his dearest friend shows us that he did actually set a high value on it. He may not have looked for a poet's immortality; he was far more concerned with the immortality promised to every Christian soul; but he was too good an artist to be ignorant of the merit of his own work.

Yet the writing of poetry, we may be sure, was not one of his major concerns. It was, like the music-making he

The Priest

so dearly loved, a solace and a joy; but it was of less consequence to him than his obligations as a parish priest. Though we may think that Walton over-emphasises the years at Bemerton and dwells too much on Herbert's achieved sanctity, we cannot suppose that Herbert himself would have wished any biographer to treat him primarily as a man of letters, relegating his priesthood to second place. After three hundred years the perspective has inevitably changed, and we set greater store by Herbert the poet than by "holy Mr. Herbert" the exemplary parish priest.

Anyone brought up in the Elizabethan courtly tradition, like George and Edward Herbert, would regard the writing of verse as one of the proper accomplishments of a cultivated man, and would attach no particular importance to it. But the exercise of creative power is inevitably a matter of great moment to every artist, however little value he may ostensibly attach to what he produces. We may be certain that for George Herbert the writing of poetry was a very great solace. His vividly personal poems are the direct result of tensions suffered and resolved; the subjective value of others lies in the play of the fancy and the exercise of technical skill. Before he became a priest, Herbert's life, though, sober, was not severely disciplined; but at Bemerton he imposed certain rules upon himself and practised mortification. Increasingly, the writing of poetry must have become a source of relief. He was far too civilized a man to deny himself the pleasure of poetry and music; indeed, he so arranged his time that he could regularly enjoy music-making; but both these delights belonged to his leisure hours.

It was to music that Herbert turned when he wanted to escape completely from anxiety and inner conflict. These he could express in his poetry, and so to some extent free himself from them; but in music he could forget them entirely. Aubrey mentions that "he had a very good hand on the lute

George Herbert

and sett his own lyricks or sacred poems".[1] At Bemerton he was only a mile from Salisbury, and in Walton's words, "though he was a lover of retiredness, yet his love to *Musick* was such, that he usually went twice every week on certain appointed days, to the *Cathedral Church* in *Salisbury*; and at his return would say, *That his time spent in Prayer, and Cathedral Musick, elevated his Soul, and was his Heaven upon Earth.* But before his return thence to *Bemerton,* he would usually sing and play his part, at an appointed private Musick-meeting; and, to justifie this practice, he would often say, *Religion does not banish mirth, but only moderates, and sets rules to it*" (p. 303).

The most delightful of all Walton's anecdotes concerns this same group of music-makers, and deserves to be quoted at length: "In another walk to *Salisbury,* he saw a poor man, with a poorer horse, that was fall'n under his Load; they were both in distress, and needed present help; which Mr. *Herbert* perceiving, put off his Canonical Coat, and help'd the poor man to unload, and after, to load his horse: the poor man blest him for it: and he blest the poor man; and was so like the good *Samaritan,* that he gave him money to refresh both himself and his horse; and told him, *That if he lov'd himself, he should be merciful to his Beast.* Thus he left the poor man, and at his coming to his musical friends at *Salisbury,* they began to wonder that Mr. *George Herbert,* which us'd to be so trim and clean, came into that company so soyl'd and discompos'd; but he told them the occasion: And when one of the company told him, *He had disparag'd himself by so dirty an employment,* his answer was, *That the thought of what he had done, would prove Musick to him at Midnight* ... *And though I do not wish for the like occasion every day, yet let me tell you, I would not willingly pass one day of my life without comforting a sad soul, or shewing mercy; and I praise God for this occasion: And now let's tune our instruments*" (p. 305).

[1] *op. cit.* p. 137.

The Priest

Some seventeen years before Walton wrote his *Life*, Barnabas Oley, in his preface to the first edition of *A Priest to the Temple* (1652), had borne witness to Herbert's delight in music. Setting down the "severall excellencies of our Author", he mentions "his *conscientious* expense of Time . . . his eminent *Temperance* and *Frugality* . . . his private *Fastings*, his *mortification of the body* . . ." Besides holding the English prayer-book in high esteem, "He was moreover so great a Lover of *Church Musick*, that he usually called it *Heaven upon Earth* . . . But above all, his chief delight was in the Holy Scriptures."[1]

Oley apologises in this preface for having written so many pages about Herbert without having offered "so much as with one dash of a Pensil . . . to describe that person of his, which afforded so unusual a Contesseration of Elegancies, and Sett of Rarities to the Beholder".[2] Walton, who knew Herbert by sight, though he was not personally acquainted with him, gives this description of his appearance and manners: "He was for his person of a stature inclining towards Tallness; his Body was very strait, and so far from being cumbred with too much flesh, that he was lean to an extremity. His aspect was chearful, and his speech and motion did both declare him a Gentleman; for they were so meek and obliging, that they purchased love and respect from all that knew him" (p. 285).

There is every reason to suppose that Herbert was happy in his work at Bemerton, for only a man who had experienced the satisfactions of a country parson's life could have written *A Priest to the Temple*; but his spirit was more susceptible than ever to signs of his divine Master's favour or disfavour. Anyone believing as fervently as Herbert that God is love is exposed to refinements of suffering when things go ill with him.

[1] *op. cit.* N8.
[2] *ibid*, O5.

George Herbert

> No scrue, no piercer can
> Into a piece of timber work and winde
> As God's afflictions into man,
> When he a torture hath design'd.
>
> <div align="right">(<i>Confession</i>, p. 126).</div>

Herbert experienced many degrees of sorrow, and as many of joy; missing, because of his fundamental sanity, ecstasy at one end of the scale and despair at the other.

His spiritual condition was intimately affected by his bodily health, for the tendency to consumption reasserted itself and took increasing hold on him. What grieved him even more than his actual physical infirmity was the frustration it brought to all his dearest hopes.

> What is this strange and uncouth thing?
> To make me sigh, and seek, and faint, and die,
> Untill I had some place, where I might sing,
>   And serve thee; and not onely I,
> But all my wealth and familie might combine
> To set thy honour up, as our designe.
>
> And then when after much delay,
> Much wrastling, many a combate, this deare end,
> So much desir'd, is giv'n, to take away
>   My power to serve thee; to unbend
> All my abilities, my designes confound
> And lay my threatnings bleeding on the ground.
>
> One ague dwelleth in my bones,
> Another in my soul (the memorie
> What I would do for thee, if once my grones
>   Could be allow'd for harmonie):
> I am in all a weak disabled thing,
> Save in the sight thereof, where strength doth sting.

The Priest

>   Besides, things sort not to my will,
> Ev'n when my will doth study thy renown:
> Thou turnest th' edge of all things on me still,
>   Taking me up to throw me down:
> So that, ev'n when my hopes seem to be sped,
> I am to grief alive, to them as dead.
>
>   To have my aim, and yet to be
> Further from it then when I bent my bow;
> To make my hopes my torture, and the fee
>   Of all my woes another wo,
> Is in the midst of delicates to need,
> And ev'n in Paradise to be a weed.
>
> (The Crosse, p. 164).

Yet even this poignant lament ends with words of acceptance and submission:

>   Ah my deare Father, ease my smart!
> These contrarieties crush me: these crosse actions
> Doe winde a rope about, and cut my heart:
>   And yet since these thy contradictions
> Are properly a crosse felt by thy Sonne,
> With but four words, my words, *Thy will be done.*

As if to counterpoise this poem, the one that immediately follows it in *The Temple* begins:

>   How fresh, O Lord, how sweet and clean
>   Are thy returns! ev'n as the flowers in spring.

And nothing that Herbert ever wrote is more typical of him than the stanza in this same poem:

>   And now in age I bud again,
>   After so many deaths I live and write;
>   I once more smell the dew and rain,

George Herbert

> And relish versing: O my onely light,
> It cannot be
> That I am he
> On whom thy tempests fell all night.
>
> *(The Flower, p. 165).*

When finally physical death came to him, he met it serenely. Walton's account of his last days and hours was taken from eye-witnesses, Edmond Duncon and Arthur Woodnoth. Duncon, in recounting the story of his visits to Herbert, expressly said that the looks, behaviour and words of the dying man made such an impression on him that after almost forty years they remained fresh in his memory.

Arthur Woodnoth, Herbert's "old and dear friend", was with him during the last weeks of his life, and was present at his death-bed. To him, presumably, Walton owes the story of Herbert's last Sunday, when he rose from his bed, called for one of his instruments, tuned it, and then played and sang his own joyous verses in praise of Sunday. "And thus", says Walton, "he continued meditating, and praying, and rejoicing, till the day of his death" (p. 317).

Towards the end, he fell into a sudden agony; and when his wife besought him to tell her what ailed him, he replied "That he had past a Conflict with his last Enemy, and had overcome him, by the merits of his Master Jesus." Then, seeing her and his nieces weeping "to an extremity", he begged them if they loved him, to withdraw into the next room and pray there for him, "for nothing but their lamentations could make his death uncomfortable... They yielded him a sad obedience, leaving only with him Mr. *Woodnot* and Mr. *Bostock*". Herbert then delivered his will to his old friend Woodnoth, who promised to act as executor and to care for the welfare of Mrs. Herbert and the two surviving nieces. Then, with a prayer on his lips, George Herbert died,

The Priest

breathing forth "his Divine Soul, without any apparent disturbance" (p. 318).

The day of his death was Friday, March 1st, 1633, and he was buried two days later, on Quinquagesima Sunday, in his little church at Bemerton. According to Aubrey, whose uncle, Thomas Danvers, was at the funeral, he "was buryed (according to his owne desire) with the singing service for the buriall of the dead, by the singing men of Salisbury . . . he lyes in the chancell, under no large, nor yet very good, marble grave-stone, without any inscription".[1] To this day, there is only a small tablet let into the chancel wall, with the initials G. H., to mark where George Herbert's mortal remains were buried.

His wife, after about six years of widowhood, married Sir Robert Cook, of Highnam in Gloucestershire, and bore him a daughter. According to Walton, many of Herbert's private writings had been preserved by his wife, and she had intended to make them public, but they were destroyed when Highnam House was burnt during the Civil War. She survived her second husband by about fifteen years, and died in 1663, thirty years after the death of George Herbert.

When he died, Herbert was not yet forty. He had been a country parson for less than three years, yet the people around Salisbury, in his brother Edward's words, held him "little less than sainted". The publication of *The Temple* in the year following his death added immeasurably to his reputation. Not only were the poems an inspiration to other poets; they were read and loved by people as unlike as King Charles and the puritan divine Richard Baxter. It was Baxter, indeed, who hit upon the secret of Herbert's enduring appeal as a Christian poet: "*Herbert* speaks *to God* like one that *really believeth a God*, and whose business in this world is

[1] *op. cit.* p. 137.

George Herbert

most *with God*. *Heart-work* and *Heaven-work* make up his books."[1]

Implicit faith of this kind is sometimes supposed to be the prerogative of simple souls. Herbert's faith, ultimately, was childlike in its responsiveness; but his was not a simple character. His subtle, self-searching poems enable us to know, with extraordinary intimacy, his moods, his likes and dislikes, his convictions, his hopes; and the record of his life shows him a man subject to conflicting impulses, and unable for many years to resolve the struggle. Intellectually gifted, charming, fastidious, able to shine among men of the world, he was finally capable of consecrating his whole life to the service of God. The drama was an interior one; there is nothing spectacular about the achievements of George Herbert, whether as man or poet; but in both capacities, his striving for perfection earned him immortality.

[1] Preface to *Poetical Fragments*, 1681. Quoted by Hutchinson, *Works*, p. xliv.

III

Literary Remains

AT the time of George Herbert's death no English writings of his were in print, and only a few of the Latin poems which he had written at Cambridge had been published. These included his elegy on Henry, Prince of Wales, written when he was nineteen, the same age as the young prince, who died in 1612; his elegy on Bacon, printed in the year of the Lord Chancellor's death; and the series of poems in honour of his mother, which were published together with Donne's obituary sermon a bare month after her death in 1627. His most famous Latin poem, also addressed to Bacon, *In Honorem D. D. Verulamij*, etc., circulated in manuscript, and so did his *Responsoriae*, probably written about the time that he became Public Orator. This series of reproofs against Andrew Melville, the eminent Scottish presbyterian, may have been occasioned by the reprinting in 1620 of his diatribe against the ceremonies of the Church of England, *Anti-Tami-Cami-Categoria*. Walton suggests that Herbert wrote these Latin verses while he was still at Westminster. At all events, they won him a certain fame among his fellow Anglicans. Other Latin poems were published in 1652 in the volume *Herbert's Remains*.

Some of his English poems must also have circulated in manuscript before his death, for his contemporaries knew him as a poet as well as a scholar. We have no evidence as to which of his poems were known during his life-time, though *The Church Militant*, from its unlikeness in technique

George Herbert

and tone to Herbert's other poems, looks like an early work, possibly belonging to his Cambridge period.

The manuscript of his collected poems was conveyed at his death to his friend Nicholas Ferrar, who caused a copy to be made by one of the Little Gidding amanuenses. He sent this copy to the University authorities at Cambridge to obtain their license for the printing of the book. This was not obtained without question. To quote Walton: "the Vice-Chancellor would by no means allow the two so much noted Verses,

> *Religion stands an Tip-toe in our Land,*
> *Ready to pass to the American Strand.*

to be printed; and Mr. *Farrer* would by no means allow the Book to be printed, and want them: But after some time, and some arguments, for and against their being made publick, the Vice-Chancellor said, *I knew Mr.* Herbert *well, and know that he had many heavenly Speculations, and was a Divine Poet: but I hope the World will not take him to be an inspired Prophet, and therefore I License the whole book:* So that it came to be printed, without the diminution or addition of a syllable, since it was deliver'd into the hands of Mr. *Duncon*, save only, that Mr. *Farrer* hath added that excellent Preface that is printed before it" (315).

The fair copy made at Little Gidding, with the signatures of the licensers, is in the Bodleian Library.[1] It corresponds very closely with the first edition of *The Temple, Sacred Poems and Private Ejaculations,* which was printed in 1633, within a year of Herbert's death, by Thomas Buck and Roger Daniel, printers to the University of Cambridge. What became of the original manuscript is, unhappily, not known.

There is another manuscript collection of Herbert's poems

---

[1] MS Tanner 307. It belonged at one time to Abp. Sancroft.

Literary Remains

extant, in Dr. William's Library, Gordon Square, London.[1] This little book contains only sixty-nine of the poems printed in *The Temple*, though there are six poems in it which do not appear in the published collection. There is no title-page and no author's name, and the English poems are all in the handwriting of a copyist. Two groups of Latin poems, however, entitled *Passio Discerpta* and *Lucus*, are in George Herbert's own hand; and the same beautiful script is to be seen in the corrections and emendations to some of the English poems. Clearly the book represents an earlier collection of Herbert's verse than the one he sent to Nicholas Ferrar; yet this manuscript too, as a pencilled note in it records, "came originally from the Family of Little Gidding, and was probably bound there".

This Williams MS is in all likelihood a selection of the poems which Herbert wrote before he went to Bemerton; none of the specifically priestly poems are contained in it. It affords fascinating evidence of Herbert's scrupulous judgment in correcting and selecting his writings. Many of the poems in the Williams MS differ considerably in their original form from the versions in which they eventually appear in the Bodleian MS; and the six rejected poems are undoubtedly inferior to the verses on similar themes which replaced them.

Herbert may well have kept this little manuscript book by him until the end of his life, when by the agency of either Duncon or Woodnoth it was conveyed to Little Gidding. It came into the possession of one Hugh Mapletoft, rector of All Saints, Huntingdon, whose grandmother was Susanna Ferrar, sister to Nicholas; and he passed it on to another Huntingdonshire parson, one John Jones, who was interested in the history of Little Gidding. Jones surmised that this book might be the very one "sent by Mr. Herbert a little before his death to Mr. Nic. Ferrar". Even a hasty com-

[1] MS Jones B62.

George Herbert

parison of its contents with *The Temple* as issued under Ferrar's editorship would have convinced him of the impossibility of this being so.

Since the original manuscript book entrusted to Duncon has not survived, we cannot know for certain whether Ferrar as editor simply reproduced the original as it stood, or whether he was responsible for the title and the final order of the poems. In either case, he discharged his trust with very great care. *The Temple* won immediate success, and four editions were published within three years.

Herbert's only other important English work, *A Priest to the Temple*, was also in the hands of Ferrar's friends and emissaries, Duncon and Woodnoth; but for some unknown reason it was not published till 1652, nearly twenty years after Herbert's death. It made its appearance in a volume entitled *Herbert's Remains, Or, Sundry Pieces of that sweet Singer of the Temple, Mr. George Herbert, Now exposed to publick Light.* It was printed in London, by T. Maxey for Timothy Garthwait, at the little North door of St. Paul's. The major part of this volume, a very small one, is taken up by *A Priest to the Temple*. It includes a *Prefatory View of the Life of Mr. Geo. Herbert*, which Barnabas Oley acknowledged as his when a second edition of *A Priest to The Temple* was issued in 1671. In the *Remains* volume there are also Herbert's prayers before and after sermon, three of his Latin poems, and a collection of proverbs from foreign sources entitled *Jacula Prudentum*, which seems to have been put in as an afterthought, and to be only doubtfully attributable to Herbert. He was probably the compiler of a large collection of "Outlandish Proverbs" which appeared in 1640, bound up in a volume entitled *Witts Recreations*. The bibliographical evidence about the collections of proverbs is admirably presented by Canon Hutchinson.[1]

[1] *Works of George Herbert*, pp. 568–573.

Literary Remains

It seems strange that *A Priest to the Temple,* or *The Country Parson,* to use its more familiar sub-title, should not have been published soon after Herbert's death, before the outbreak of the Civil War, rather than in 1652 when, under Cromwell's dictatorship, faithful pastors of the Anglican church were forced to minister and preach in secret. In the preface to the second edition, which appeared after the Restoration, Barnabas Oley openly assumed the responsibility for the previous edition, congratulating himself upon his courage in having emulated Ezra, Nehemiah and Daniel in publishing the book in 1652, "in that Day, when violence was at the Height".

The original preface, relegated in the second edition to the back of the book, was addressed "To the Christian, more designedly, to the *Clergy* Reader", and it begins "My poor and dear Brother". The editor dwells upon the tribulations of the times, admitting however that some of the clergy by their deficiencies had brought misfortune on their own heads. On the 1671 preface, Oley makes a special appeal to the younger clergy, some "not born before the Troubles broke forth", reminding them "what a Halcyonian Calm, a Blessed Time of Peace, this Church of England had for many years, above all the Churches in the world besides".[1] He reflects that the publication of *The Country Parson* might either incite the Restoration clergy to better living, or the laity to dissatisfaction with their ministers; and he expresses a general longing on the part of the "Old Clergy of the Nation" to conform to Herbert's ideals. The book was reprinted in 1675, and a fourth edition came out in 1701; there was then an interval of over a hundred years before it was reprinted.

Since *A Priest to the Temple* contains a preface by Herbert

---

[1] The preface is not paginated in the 1671 edition, but this remark occurs in the third paragraph.

George Herbert

himself, dated 1632, it is clear that he intended it for publication, though he contemplated the addition of points by other hands "untill the Book grow to a compleat Pastorall". Apparently the manuscript remained in the hands of Edmond Duncon for many years, since it was he, by Oley's testimony, who handed it to the printer. Walton says that it was in the possession of Woodnoth, but he may have bequeathed it to Duncon. Why it was not printed promptly remains a mystery.

There is considerable evidence that George Herbert was responsible for the collection of over a thousand proverbs from French, Spanish and Italian sources, which (as already noted) appeared in 1640 in a compilation *Witts Recreation* under the title *Outlandish Proverbs selected by Mr. G. H.* The likelihood is that he made his own translations of a large proportion of these proverbs and maxims. The collection therefore represents no small expenditure of time and trouble; but Herbert's fondness for proverbial wisdom, exemplified in his poetry and prose, lends colour to the idea that he undertook it as a hobby and pastime.

Some of the outlandish proverbs are utilized in his writings. In *Confession*, for instance, he adapts No. 475, "Wealth is like rheume, it falles on the weakest parts". In the poem the comparison is applied to the afflictions sent by God:

> They are too subtill for the subt'llest hearts;
> And fall, like rheumes, upon the tendrest parts.
> (p. 126).

Not very many of the proverbs in this collection have become acclimatized; regrettably, when one considers such pleasantly trenchant adages as No. 321, "Bee not a Baker, if your head be of butter", or "It's no sure rule to fish with a cros-bow" (No. 293). Quite a number, however, correspond with proverbs of English origin. "The scalded dog feares cold water" (No. 13), for instance, is a rather more penetrating version of "The burnt child dreads the fire".

In 1634, a year after Herbert's death, a volume entitled *Hygiasticon* was printed at Cambridge. It contained, besides the tract by Lessius which gave its name to the volume, *A Treatise of Temperance and Sobrietie,* translated by George Herbert from Lessius' Latin version of Luigi Cornaro's *Trattato de la vita sobria* (Padua, 1558). The preface describes how "Master George Herbert of blessed memorie, having at the request of a Noble Personage translated it into English, sent a copie thereof, not many moneths before his death, unto some friends of his, who a good while before had given an attempt of regulating themselves in matter of *Diet*".

The nobleman was probably Bacon, who in his *Historia Vitae et Mortis* calls attention to Cornaro's treatise and practice; and the friends interested in diet were almost certainly the Ferrars. Nicholas Ferrar was associated with the publication of *Hygiasticon,* and if he did not himself translate Lessius' Latin tract, he seems to have commissioned the translation. Canon Hutchinson points out[1] that he was the likelier to be interested in Cornaro since, during his travels in Italy as a young man, he had fallen dangerously ill at Padua, Cornaro's own city, where a very old physician persuaded him that he was his own best doctor, and that he would daily improve in health if he would observe a regularity in his diet. We know from Walton that Herbert tried to cure himself of his constitutional weakness by a spare diet, and that while staying with his brother Henry at Woodford he "became his own physician and cured himself of his Ague" (284). Whether he undertook the translation of Cornaro at Bemerton or earlier is not known.

Still another of his literary remains links him with Nicholas

[1] *Works,* p. 565.

George Herbert

Ferrar. This is his commendatory letter and brief notes on Valdesso's *Considerations,* sent him by Ferrar, who had made a translation from an Italian version of the Spanish original. Ferrar was presumably doubtful about the acceptability of some of Valdesso's views to authorities of the Church of England, and the book did in fact incur the censure of Dr. Thomas Jackson, President of Corpus Christi College, Oxford, who examined the work on behalf of the Vice-Chancellor before it was issued by the university printer in 1638, some months after Ferrar's own death. Herbert's annotations evidently weighed with Dr. Jackson, for he mentions them as mitigating the offensiveness of certain passages. These notes were sent by Herbert to Ferrar in September 1632. They show that, although he abhorred the chop-logic of religious controversy, he was well able to write discerningly on points of doctrine. His letter to Ferrar is typically generous in its enthusiasm for Valdesso's understanding of the Gospel, and especially for his devotion "towards our deare Master and Lord . . . for which I doe so love him, that were there nothing else, I would Print it, that with it the honour of my Lord might be published" (p. 305).

Three Orations and sixteen letters written during Herbert's period of office at Cambridge are printed in the Oxford edition of his Works. Two other Latin letters are also included; one to Bishop Lancelot Andrewes and the other to Robert Creighton, who succeeded Herbert as Public Orator and, after his death, as prebend of Leighton Ecclesia in Lincoln Cathedral.

Nineteen of Herbert's English letters are extant, but only two have survived in his own hand. Our debt to Izaak Walton on this score is great, for he printed no less than eleven of these letters in various editions of his *Life*. They fall into two groups, the Cambridge and the Bemerton letters; and though they offer only fragmentary evidence about Herbert's activities, they shed considerable light on his disposition, and witness to the change that took place in him when he renounced the world for the church.

George Herbert's fame rests on two books only, *The Temple* and *A Priest to the Temple*. The poems immeasurably outshine the little pastoral treatise; but this would hold its own as a study of seventeenth-century religious ideals and practice even if our interest in its author were not already so deeply engaged by his poetry. It will be discussed in a separate chapter; here it may suffice to say that it bears many signs of incompleteness. There is no orderly progression from chapter to chapter, and though Herbert furnished it with a preface, he was evidently conscious of its unfinished character.

Nor does *The Temple* give the impression of a completed book. Although some of the poems have been so arranged as to suggest a deliberate structure, the scheme is actually a very elusive one, and they tend to fall into small groups, related tenuously if at all. Mortal sickness cut short Herbert's writing of poetry; and it is his early death that accounts for the illogicalities and lacunae in the framework of *The Temple*.

Whether Herbert himself or Nicholas Ferrar provided it with its sub-title, *Sacred Poems and Private Ejaculations*, we have no means of knowing; but it is interesting that the two categories should have been distinguished from the first. The poems are not sorted out into public and private groups; but the sub-title at least indicates that the scope of the book is wide and its author's intentions complex.

It falls into three sections, each distinguished in the first edition by special page-headings: *The Church Porch*, *The Church*, *The Church Militant*. Except on the title-page, *The Temple* does not appear.[1] The opening and closing poems

---

[1] Aubrey, *op. cit.* p. 137 notes "*Scripsit*. Sacred Poems, called *The Church*, printed, Cambridge, 1633: a Booke entitled *The Country Parson*, not printed till about 1650, 8vo."

differ very markedly in style and tone from the body of lyrics that forms the core of the book.

The Church Militant, written in heroic couplets, a metre that Herbert does not use elsewhere, seems from internal evidence, including its strong anti-Roman bias, to be a comparatively early work; and its satiric tone strengthens this conjecture. It is reminiscent of Donne both in manner and in choice of subject.

The ever-westward progress of the Christian religion is traced from its origins in Palestine through Alexandria and Byzantium to Rome, and thence to protestant Germany and England. Herbert observes that the westward drift is still operative, for the imperfection of the reformation in Europe may mean that Religion will

> "to *America* flee;
> They have their times of Gospel, ev'n as we . . ." (p. 197).

Herbert is not, however, so optimistic as his contemporary Dr. William Twisse[1] who wrote in 1634 to his friend Joseph Mede: "And then considering our English plantations of late, and the opinion of many grave divines concerning the Gospel fleeing westward, sometimes I have had such thoughts, why may not that be the place of the New Jerusalem?" Herbert more soberly remarks:

> Yet as the Church shall thither westward flie,
> So Sin shall trace and dog her instantly. (p. 197).

He has already charted the journey of Sin, who follows closely in Religion's wake, perverting the faith wherever he finds it, and achieving his greatest triumph in Rome. Here he caricatures the three offices of Christ, as prophet, priest

[1] Quoted by Canon Hutchinson, *Works*, p. 547.

and king, and employs the deceptions typical of all the civilizations through which he has travelled.

> From *Egypt* he took pettie deities,
> From *Greece* oracular infallibilities,
> And from old *Rome* the libertie of pleasure
> By free dispensings of the Churches treasure.   (p. 195).

It is a vigorous poem, clearly conceived and elaborately worked out; but if Herbert made other experiments in this vein, he did not preserve them. His bent was not for satire, nor was he as interested as Donne in the politics of divided christendom.

The Church Porch also belongs to a period earlier than the main body of poems in *The Temple*. Herbert seems to have kept it by him, revising it from time to time. Its stanza and its didactic tone give it a strongly Elizabethan flavour:

> Wit's an unruly engine, wildly striking
> Sometimes a friend, sometimes the engineer;
> Hast thou the knack? pamper it not with liking:
> But if thou want it, buy it not too deere.
>   Many, affecting wit beyond their power,
>   Have got to be a deare fool for an hour.   (p. 16).

It is a long, rambling poem, full of good advice which is given in a forthright, homely way. Reading it, we are constantly reminded of Herbert's fondness for proverbs. His admonitions are conveyed pithily and with little display of emotion, as proverbial wisdom always is conveyed:

> "Who aimeth at the sky
> Shoots higher much then he that means a tree."   (p. 19).

> "A good digestion turneth all to health."   (p. 20).

George Herbert

"Kneeling ne're spoil'd silk stocking" (p. 22), (as untrue a line as Herbert ever wrote); "Slacknesse breeds wormes" (p. 20), "Never was scraper brave man" (p. 12)—examples could be multiplied endlessly. *The Church Porch* is addressed to readers not much inclined to godliness by a preacher not unacquainted with worldliness. Its position at the beginning of the book is, obviously, deliberate. Lay matters can properly be discussed in the church porch, and warnings given of how to behave in the house of God.

The arrangement of the first few poems in *The Temple* strongly suggests that one of Herbert's intentions was to take his readers on an imaginary itinerary round a church building. Following *The Church Porch* comes a page headed *Superliminare,* which contains two quatrains. The first of these, in the Williams MS, appears on a page to itself, with the title *Perirranterium,* and this formidable word, the Greek equivalent of the Latin Aspergillium or holy-water sprinkler, appears (differently spelt) in the Bodleian MS as a sub-title to *The Church Porch*. It is more appropriate to the quatrain:

> Thou, whom the former precepts have
> Sprinkled and taught, how to behave
> Thyself in church: approach, and taste
> The churches mysticall repast. (p. 25).

Wherever Herbert intended the word to stand, it is clear that his wish was to remind the reader of the necessity for pausing at the threshold of a holy place, and of the sanctification of worshippers symbolised by the holy water. All these verses serve to prepare the approach to the central section of the book, The Church; and once we are over the threshold, the atmosphere immediately changes; we are on hallowed ground.

In *The Country Parson* Herbert describes how the priest

goes into the church, "at his first entrance humbly adoring, and worshipping the invisible majesty and presence of Almighty God" (p. 236). Similarly, he directs the attention of his readers, on their first entry into his collection of sacred poems, to *The Altar*. (This, incidentally, is one of the very few pieces in which Herbert indulged the fashionable fancy for constructing a poem in imitation of the shape of its subject.) Following on *The Altar* comes, logically enough, *The Sacrifice*; but since this poem is a dramatic monologue of Christ on the cross, it may have as much to do with the rood screen as with the eucharistic sacrifice. Stemming from this, the thought of the Passion dominates the next groups of poems, and the journey round the church is for a while abandoned, though later in the book we find poems on *Church Monuments, Church Lock and Key, The Church Floor* and *The Windows*.

Another project in Herbert's mind was certainly that of celebrating the Christian year with poems on the major feasts and recurring seasons; but this too is incomplete. There are poems on Christmas, Lent, Good Friday, Easter and Whit Sunday, on Trinity Sunday and the feast of St. Mary Magdalene, his mother's patron, besides a poem *To All Angels and Saints*; but even if we include poems on the sacraments and services of the church, the yearly round has not been adequately covered.

The deficiencies in both these schemes evidently struck Christopher Harvey, another country parson and a devoted admirer of Herbert, who in 1640 published *The Synagogue, or The Shadow of the Temple, in imitation of Mr. George Herbert*. This collection of verses was often included in subsequent editions of *The Temple*, presumably because the completion of Herbert's two projects commended itself to readers. Harvey wrote on The Church-Yard, The Church-Stile, The Church-Gate, The Church Walls, Church Utensils, the Reading-Pew, The Pulpit, The Communion-Table ("Some call't

George Herbert

the Altar, some the holy Table, The name I stick not at") and Communion Plate. He also completed the Christian Year scheme, occasionally achieving a really good poem, and he added a painstaking series on Church Officers, to include the Sexton, the Clerk, the Church Warden and the Overseer of the Poor, besides Bishop, Priest and Deacon. *The Synagogue* also contains verses that come into the category of "private ejaculations", and some of these, though derivative, are unaffectedly devout in feeling and gracefully phrased.

Herbert's scope was, however, far wider than Harvey's or, in a later age, Keble's. "The Church" is the title set on every page-heading of the main portion of his book, and its true subject is that mysterious institution which, in spite of all its human shortcomings, still remains the safeguard of the divine mysteries and the dispenser of comfort to the faithful.

Although the church in which Herbert was born and bred had but recently seceded from Rome, it had preserved (to its own satisfaction, at any rate) the idea of Ecclesia. The Anglicans continued to offer up corporate prayer for "the holy Church universal", and one of the several collects in the Book of Common Prayer which invoke God's mercy on his Church refers to it in a phrase that seems to accord particularly well with Herbert's own way of regarding it: "Lord, we beseech thee to keep *thy household the Church* in continual godliness."

Herbert's spirit delighted in the order, the beauty and the fellowship implicit in the idea of the Church; for though he had his share of pride and stubbornness of will, he was not a natural rebel, but one of those humble enough to find reassurance in associating themselves with other souls in traditional forms of worship. Whether, therefore, he writes as a priest, teaching and preaching, or as an individual Christian, in moods of despondency or joy, he can set all his poems within the context of the Church; for the intercourse between

Literary Remains

the single, searching soul and her divine Master is part of the eternal intercourse between Christ and his Church.

Reverting to the distinction, noted earlier, between sacred poems and private ejaculations, it may be remarked that a great many poems in *The Temple,* besides those on church festivals and church features, are public rather than private in their intention. Though Herbert's tone is seldom didactic, a number of his poems are exhortations of one kind or another. Sometimes, as in *Miserie,* he uses the rhetorical cunning of a preacher who knows how to keep his congregation's attention by sudden questions, apt comparisons, raillery:

> Man cannot serve thee; let him go,
> And serve the swine: there, there is his delight:
> He doth not like this vertue, no;
> Give him his dirt to wallow in all night:
> These Preachers make
> His head to shoot and ake. (p. 101).

In *Providence* he speaks explicitly as a priest, enumerating the marvels of the created world and extolling the divine economy that sustains them. The many poems on virtues and vices are didactic in intent, reflective in tone. Sometimes, as in *The Pulley,* he uses the method of parable; sometimes, as in *Humilitie,* that of allegory. *Vanitie* is a beautifully worked out argument, *Man* another.

Nor can the occasional acrostics, anagrams and similar ingenuities be described as "private ejaculations", while a number of lyrics patently written for music are no more "personal" than any typical Elizabethan verse from a song-book.

There remain, however, the poems which we today, with our insatiable interest in the psychology of the individual, value above the rest; the poems in which Herbert speaks in his own person. In some he reflects upon the past or present

George Herbert

circumstances of his own life, in others he records a passing mood or addresses a heartfelt cry to God. The directly autobiographical poems have been drawn on liberally in the two preceding chapters. Quite as revealing of Herbert's personality are such poems as *Employment ii*, in which his impatience finds expression; or *The Method*, where he accounts for God's apparent indifference to his prayers by finding evidence of his own indifference to God; or *Unkindnesse*, in which he contrasts the courtesy he uses to human friends with his neglect of the divine Lover of souls.

Somewhere between the intensely personal poems and the moralizing ones come those lyrics which are peculiarly characteristic of Herbert in the range of English religious verse; poems in which a spiritual situation is dramatized, the poet himself participating and speaking in the first person, though the other actors and the setting belong to the world of parable. *The Pilgrimage* and *Peace* are fine examples of this genre, and there are several briefer parables conveyed through dialogue or brisk action:

> I gave to Hope a watch of mine; but he
> An anchor gave to me . . .
> *(Hope*, p. 121).

or:

> Meeting with Time, Slack thing, said I,
> Thy sithe is dull; whet it for shame.
> *(Time*, p. 122).

These poems have not the poignancy of the personal confessions, but they are immediate and telling; and *Love*, which belongs to this category, is one of the most perfect religious poems in the English language. The successful use of this convention depends upon the poet having thoroughly mastered his originating emotion, so that he can to some extent externalize his experience and make it valid for others. The "I" in such poems refers to Herbert, but not exclusively; it includes his fellow-christians too.

> Love bade me welcome: yet my soul drew back,
>   Guiltie of dust and sinne.
> But quick-ey'd Love, observing me grow slack
>   From my first entrance in,
> Drew nearer to me, sweetly questioning
>   If I lack'd any thing.
>
> A guest, I answer'd, worthy to be here:
>   Love said, You shall be he.
> I the unkinde, ungratefull? Ah my deare,
>   I cannot look on thee.
> Love took my hand, and smiling did reply,
>   Who made the eyes but I?
>
> Truth Lord, but I have marr'd them: let my shame
>   Go where it doth deserve.
> And know you not, sayes Love, who bore the blame?
>   My deare, then I will serve.
> You must sit down, sayes Love, and taste my meat:
>   So I did sit and eat.
>   (*Love iii*, p. 188).

The sense of fellowship that enabled Herbert to make his "I" inclusive did not derive from any natural bonhomie or expansiveness but from his devotion to the Church, the household of faith. People to whom the very idea of a Church is inimical will not make much of George Herbert's poetry. But it must be admitted that the source of his strength was the source of his weakness too. Any post-reformation poet is bound to be hampered by a close attachment to one particular branch of the Christian church. Not only is this allegiance cramping to his imagination, it gives his language a smack of

George Herbert

provincialism. Visionaries and mystics are unhampered by definite creeds and speak a universal language; churchmen proceed with greater caution.

George Herbert was not a mystic. He was a practising Christian, passionately sincere and devout in his latter years, but essentially a man of action, not a contemplative. Though he achieved a rare saintliness of character, there is nothing in his writings or in the record of his life to suggest that he experienced abnormal raptures or desolations, or that he ever had sudden blinding glimpses of hidden truths. Some of his poems are deliberately the utterances of a priest, and these, like similar poems by Hopkins, are likely to alienate readers to whom orthodox Christianity is either incomprehensible or unacceptable. But when Herbert and Hopkins (so strikingly alike in temperament and in their experience of the baffling ways of God) set aside their professional preoccupations and write as human souls, the fact that they express themselves in religious terms need not be a serious obstacle to sympathetic understanding. When they grapple with moods of discouragement or irresolution, or express the joy of hope renewed, they are treating of matters that fall within the ambit of the ordinary man, and he can penetrate their meaning.

IV

The Country Parson

BEFORE attempting a fuller consideration of the themes and imagery of the poems in *The Temple*, or an assessment of Herbert's originality as a poet, it may be as well to deal with his pastoral treatise, *A Priest to the Temple*. Though it belongs to the years at Bemerton, whereas many of the poems were written before he went there, it is not necessary to insist upon chronology. Not only was Herbert's whole literary output very small, it was singularly consistent. He himself must have been aware of this, for a comparison of the Williams MS with the final volume shows that he worked his earlier pieces in among the later ones according to their literary suitability, without regard to when they were written.

A Priest to the Temple was published, as has already been noted, nearly twenty years after Herbert's death. The fact that it came out at an unpropitious time for the launching of a handbook of Anglican pastoral practice may account for the way in which the title-page is set out; for this suggests that the book was commended to the public as a Character Sketch, a "manuscript portrait" of an idealized kind. The page reads "A Priest to the Temple or The Countrey Parson, His Character and Rule of Holy Life", and the word Character is emphasized by being given a line to itself and large capital letters. It is conceivable that Herbert had in mind an extended essay on the Theophrastian model, for the genre was popular when he wrote his little book. *Microcosmographie* had appeared in 1628, and the temper of Earle's sketches, sober and reflective, rather resembles Herbert's own. It seems likelier, however, that when George Herbert was drafting *The Country Parson* he had no thought of "the common reader" in his mind.

The intention of the book is made clear in the preface, where he explains that he is setting down the ideals of priestly and pastoral conduct, towards which he himself was aiming. The readers he contemplates are his fellow clergy, "who may not despise my poor labours, but add to those points, which I have observed, untill the Book grow to a compleat Pastorall" (224). It is essentially a practical treatise, in which Herbert explores the methods by which a contemporary parson could strengthen the hold of the established church upon the hearts and minds of the people of rural England.

Nearly a hundred years had passed since the Supremacy Act of 1534 marked the secession of the English Church from the Church of Rome. Politico-religious questions during that century had been the cause of incessant troubles and tensions; yet the Church of England managed, in that comparatively brief period, to consolidate its position in the most remarkable manner. The skill of Cranmer and his adjutants in reducing the medieval service-books to one English prayer-book, Matthew Parker's statesmanship and scholarship, Richard Hooker's temperate and closely-reasoned arguments in defence of the *via media*, Lancelot Andrewes' example as an episcopal administrator and as a preacher inspired by the purest devotion —these were some of the factors which established the Church of England as something quite other than a protestant sect. It claimed to be a reformed branch of the church, and the harvest of devotional literature which it produced in the seventeenth century is the finest substantiation of that claim.

The Reformation in England, though it was marred by some disgraceful incidents, such as the sacking of the monasteries and the execution of Sir Thomas More, was not inspired by hostility to the doctrines or the traditions of the Catholic

The Country Parson

Church. Within the Church of England, liturgical worship went on and the succession of bishops was unbroken. A purified Catholic tradition was what the best Anglicans aimed at; and the Laudian church did not fall far short of that mark.

Educated English churchmen of Herbert's generation were naturally aware of the Counter-Reformation and of the astonishing manifestation (material as well as spiritual) of piety that it had called forth. Edward Herbert, who visited Rome in 1614, must have brought back news of the completion of the new St. Peter's, of the great Jesuit buildings, the Gesù and the Collegio Romano, and of a host of other churches springing up to testify to the new vigour of Catholicism. He certainly cannot be cited as a typical Anglican, but it is perhaps worth remarking that when he paid a visit to the English College (as Milton did some twenty-five years later) he observed to the Rector (a Jesuit) that he "conceived the points agreed upon both sides are greater bonds of amitie betwixt us, than that the points disagreed on could break them". Nicholas Ferrar, who had travelled extensively in Italy, tried at Little Gidding to establish a domestic substitute for the contemplative life of the cloister, something that England had lost to her real impoverishment; and George Herbert had as high a regard for the sacredness of the priestly office as any adherent to the Church of Rome.

In the hundred years between the secession from the Papacy and Herbert's ministry, the Anglican rites had not become an integral part of the lives of the people. The prayer-book had been twice quite drastically revised, and five differing translations of the Bible had appeared. These, however, were minor handicaps compared with the existence within the church of a very powerful faction which believed that the reforms in England had not been nearly radical enough. What with the puritan fanatics, the disrupting interlude of Mary's reign, and Elizabeth's compromises, it is scarcely surprising that the

George Herbert

country people still needed a great deal of instruction in the rudiments of their faith.

It may be noted that the puritans had hoped for another, and much more protestant, revision of the prayer-book on the accession of James I; but the Hampton Court Conference, far from abolishing the rite of Confirmation (as the puritans wished) enlarged the catechism by a series of questions and answers on the sacraments, and retained Confirmation as a "laying on of hands upon children baptized, and able to render an account of their faith according to the Catechism". Herbert's insistence on the necessity for constant catechizing has wider implications, but it is not unrelated to the emphasis in the Jacobean prayer-book on the responsibility of church-members to "render an account of their faith".

It was because the reformed liturgy was not yet really familiar to the country folk of England that Herbert lays such stress on public worship. From the testimony of Ferrar we know that he and his household set a memorable example of loyalty to the requirements of the Book of Common Prayer by their daily recital of the morning and evening offices in the little church at Bemerton. Walton records that Herbert "brought most of his Parishioners, and many Gentlemen in the Neighbourhood, constantly to make a part of his Congregation twice a day" (302).

It may, however, have been uphill work to induce this degree of devotion, for Herbert has a good deal to say about bad manners in church. The parson, having by his own example and by instruction shown his people "how to carry themselves in divine service, exacts of them all possible reverence, by no means enduring either talking, or sleeping, or gazing, or leaning, or half-kneeling, or any undutifull behaviour in them, but causing them, when they sit, or stand, or kneel, to do all in a strait, and steady posture, as attending to what is done in the Church, and every one, man and child,

The Country Parson

answering aloud both Amen, and all other answers, which are on the Clerks and peoples part to answer; which answers are to be done not in a hudling, or slubbering fashion, gaping, or scratching the head, or spitting even in the midst of their answer . . ." (231). Bad manners of another kind might be shown by the nobilty or gentry of the parish who "sometimes make it a piece of state not to come at the beginning of the service with their poor neighbours, but at mid-prayers, both to their own loss, and of theirs also who gaze upon them when they come in" (232).

Herbert's comment on this irreverent behaviour on the part of people who ought to know better reminds us that the discipline of the Laudian church was severe; but it also shows his courteous consideration for the feelings of others. The parson "by no means suffers it, but after divers gentle admonitions, if they persevere, he causes them to be presented; or if the poor Church-wardens be affrighted with their greatness . . . he presents them himself, only protesting to them, that not any ill will draws him to it, but the debt and obligation of his calling, being to obey God rather then men" (232).

Writing in an age when religious controversy was conducted with violent bitterness, Herbert quietly defends his beliefs without ever trying to put those who differ from him in the wrong. He takes his stand firmly upon the Book of Common Prayer and the Catholic traditions inherited by the Anglican church and sanctioned by its bishops. The strength of the puritan influence can be gauged by the fact that Herbert has to defend such practices as the use of the cross in baptism, kneeling to receive the sacrament of the altar, and the blessing of the people by the priest. As he says, "In the time of Popery, the priest's *Benedicite*, and his holy water were over highly valued; and now we are fallen to the clean contrary, even from superstition to coldnes, and Atheism" (286).

Herbert himself clearly had a fondness for the ancient

observances of the church. He specially mentions the rogation-tide processions, when the parish boundaries were beaten. Remarking that country people are much addicted to such pastimes, he says that for his part he would reprove as uncharitable those who refuse to take part in this "loving walking and neighbourly accompanying one another" (284). He speaks also of the adornment of the church at great festivals, when it should be "strawed and stuck with boughs, and perfumed with incense"; and he insists upon all its appointments and furniture being "decent" and befitting God's worship. Not, he points out, "as putting a holiness in the *things,* but as desiring to keep the middle way between superstition and slovenliness" (246). The middle way was as congenial to Herbert as to his contemporary Sir Thomas Browne, whose words in *Religio Medici* he would certainly have echoed: "There is no Church whose every part so squares unto my conscience; whose Articles, Constitutions and Customs seems so consonant to reason, and as it were framed to my particular Devotion, as this whereof I hold my belief, the Church of England."

The intention of *A Priest to the Temple* was primarily practical; but Herbert transcends his own aims, because he defines a pastor as nothing less than "the Deputy of Christ". All the manifold duties to his parishioners which he outlines are subordinated to this consideration. The priest must imitate Christ in his life as well as preach His word and celebrate His mysteries; and Herbert insists that whatever the parson is engaged on—whether specifically priestly duties, or entertaining his friends, or journeying, or ordering his own household—it is his constant obligation to reveal the love and justice of God towards mankind. But though Herbert urges this ideal with great earnestness, he is at the same time well aware of human frailty, and has his feet firmly on the ground.

The Country Parson

A life-time of experience seems to lie behind some of his shrewd comments on country folk and how to deal with them; yet his background was fashionable London and academic Cambridge. The clue is given in chapter xxvi. Having observed that "Country people are full of these petty injustices, being cunning to make use of another, and spare themselves," he remarks that "Scholers ought to be diligent in the observation of these, and driving of their generall Schoole rules ever to the smallest actions of Life; which while they dwell in their bookes, they will never finde; but being seated in the Countrey, and doing their duty faithfully, they will soon discover: especially if they carry their eyes ever open, and fix them on their charge, and not on their preferment" (266).

Herbert, whose previous associates had been men of influence and learning, readily accepted the limits set to his eloquence by country people "which are thick, and heavy, and hard to raise to a poynt of Zeal, and fervency, and need a mountaine of fire to kindle them" (233). When Donne preached in St. Paul's, vast congregations flocked to listen to his impassioned rhetoric. Herbert preached in a church that would scarcely hold a hundred people, and the majority of his listeners were unlettered rustics.

None of his sermons, unfortunately, survives; but in his chapter, The Parson Preaching, he laid down the principles on which he worked. He was concerned with one thing only; that his words should move his hearers to goodness by means of their unadorned sincerity. Had Herbert wished, he could have preached sermons that were witty, learned and eloquent; he had not been chosen Public Orator for nothing. But he rejected these ornaments in favour of simple holiness. Walton relates that on his first Sunday at Bemerton he "deliver'd his Sermon after a most florid manner; both with great learning and eloquence. But at the close of this Sermon, told them,

George Herbert

That should not be his constant way of Preaching, for, since Almighty God does not intend to lead men to heaven by hard Questions, he would not therefore fill their heads with unnecessary Notions; but that for their sakes, his language and his expressions should be more plain and practical in his future Sermons" (295).

It is not easy to estimate what was the effect on his poetry of his perpetual endeavours, during his years at Bemerton, to speak intelligibly to plain-spoken men. His poetic style had been formed before he became a priest, and his one didactic poem, *The Church Porch,* with its low-pitched diction and homely imagery, almost certainly belongs to an earlier period. Some of the more elaborate and ingenious poems in *The Temple* do not appear in the Williams MS, and there is always the possibility that the effort of adjusting his language to minds less lively than his own may have made him take a special pleasure in the intricacies of verse-writing. There is, however, enough evidence in the poems themselves of his striving towards a style of simple sincerity to suggest that his experiences as a preacher are related quite closely to his poetic practice.

To sanction the use of homely illustrations in teaching, Herbert turns to the example of Holy Scripture, "when it condescends to the naming of a plough, a hatchet, a bushell, leaven, boyes piping and dancing; showing that things of ordinary use are not only to serve in the way of drudgery, but to be washed and cleaned, and serve for lights even of Heavenly Truths" (257). There are plenty of images of biblical simplicity to be found in Herbert's poems; here is one used with a touch of humour:

> Mark how the fire in flints doth quiet lie,
>   Content and warm t' it self alone:
> But when it would appear to others eye,
>   Without a knock it never shone.   (*Content,* p. 68).

The Country Parson

Of God's goodness in providing night and sleep for man's refreshment, he writes:

> Thus in thy ebony box
> Thou dost inclose us, till the day
> Put our amendment in our way,
> And give new wheels to our disorder'd clocks.
>
> (*Evensong,* p. 64).

No doubt the disposition of his mind was such that images derived from practical occupations like carpentry or gardening came to him effortlessly and naturally; yet they must also have commended themselves to his judgment. "The Country Parson," he says, "is full of all knowledg. They say, it is an ill Mason that refuseth any stone; and there is no knowledg, but, in a skilfull hand, serves either positively as it is, or else to illustrate some other knowledg. He condescends even to the knowledge of tillage, and pasturage, and makes great use of them in teaching, because people by what they understand are best led to what they understand not" (228).

This last observation is the axiom underlying all his recommendations about teaching and preaching; and it also underlies his use of parable in his poems. This was a method he used increasingly, and with great resourcefulness, during his later years, and it commended itself to him because it was Christ's own way of making his meaning clear. In chapter xxiii of *The Country Parson* he observes that "Our Saviour made plants and seeds to teach the people; for he was the true householder, who bringeth out of his treasure things new and old; the old things of Philosophy, and the new of Grace; and maketh the one serve the other. And I conceive, our Saviour did this for three reasons; first, that by familiar things he might make his Doctrine slip the more easily into the heart even of the meanest. Secondly, that

George Herbert

labouring people (whom he chiefly considered) might have everywhere monuments of his Doctrine, remembring in gardens, his mustard-seed, and lillyes; in the field, his seed-corn, and tares; and so be not drowned altogether in the works of their vocation, but sometimes lift up their minds to better things, even in the midst of their pains. Thirdly, that he might set a Copy for Parsons" (261). And, Herbert might have added, for Poets.

His sonnet *Redemption* is nearest to the Gospel parables in its analogies—the tenant, the rich landlord, the granted petition; *The Pulley* embodies a fable as convincing as that of Pandora's box; in *The Pilgrimage* he anticipates Bunyan, but compresses his Christian's progress into a few vivid stanzas. There are about a dozen instances in *The Temple* of poetic parables, and they are surely connected with Herbert the preacher's insistence on making his thoughts intelligible to people who, as he says, prefer stories to "exhortations which, though earnest, yet often dy with the Sermon" (233).

Had Herbert never written poems, however, *The Country Parson* would remain a book eminently worth reading for the sake of the picture it gives of an Anglican clergyman's life in a rural parish before the Civil War. It is in many ways a highly idealized picture. Very few country parsons at that time were as comfortably circumstanced, or as well educated, as the one in Herbert's book. Only a generation earlier Shakespeare had made fun of the witless country curate, coupling him with the ignorant, pedantic schoolmaster; and no doubt in doing so he was drawing on his own Warwickshire recollections. The profession of a country clergyman was very different in Laudian days from what it was when Trollope wrote; and it was most exceptional for a man of Herbert's distinction to retire to a country parish. He and his wife had private means and were able to dispense all kinds of charitable help—financial, medical and legal—to their poorer neighbours. To help in the work of the very small parish there was always one curate, and latterly two. Herbert's portrait of a country parson is no more typical than he himself was. Yet he does not falsify the problems that confronted him. There was much ignorance to combat, and gross poverty, besides insolence, backbiting, stinginess and all the mean sins that breed in small localities. There were the sick to visit, the children to instruct, the troubled in conscience to advise and comfort, the diligent to encourage. In one respect at least the seventeenth-century parson was more fortunate than his present-day counterpart; he did not have to reckon with blank indifference, for personal salvation was still, even to the careless, a living issue.

Herbert did not question the social hierarchy of his time, taking it to be part of the disposition of Providence; but his own compassionate humanity comes out time and again in his reference to the less fortunate. He observes how harshly servants are usually treated: "Men usually think that servants for their mony are as other things that they buy, even as a piece of wood, which they may cut, or hack, or throw into the fire, and so they pay them their wages, all is well" (265). The country parson's servants, however, stand to him almost in the relation of children. He has a duty to educate them and to encourage them to set a good example in the parish.

It is in reading the chapters that deal with practical matters, like the parson's ordering of his household, or the giving of legal and medical advice to his flock, that the interval of time between ourselves and George Herbert becomes most apparent. Social conditions have so changed as to make Herbert's remarks on these topics seem quaint, though they are in fact full of good sense and charity.

In one chapter, A Parson's Surveys, he allows his scrutiny to range outside his parish to the country as a whole. This

George Herbert

has considerable historical interest, and shows that Herbert the parson had profited from his long sojourn in the great world. He gives sound counsel to landowners, their heirs and younger sons, advising them that "There is no school to a Parliament; and when (the Knight or Burgess) is there, he must not only be a morning man, but at Committees also; for there the particulars are exactly discussed, which are brought from thence to the House but in generall" (277). It is interesting to note that "The great and national sin of this Land he esteems to be Idlenesse" for in *The Church Porch* Herbert brings the same charge against his countrymen.

> O England! full of sinne, but most of sloth;
> Spit out thy flegme, and fill thy brest with glorie:
> Thy Gentrie bleats, as if thy native cloth
> Transfus'd a sheepishnesse into thy storie:
>   Not that they all are so; but that the most
>   Are gone to grasse, and in the pasture lost. (p. 10).

But it is seldom that George Herbert allows his interest to stray outside the parochial life that he had elected for himself.

How deeply his heart was engaged in his vocation can be seen from such a passage as this: "The Country Parson being to administer the Sacraments, is at a stand with himself, how or what behaviour to assume for so holy things. Especially at Communion times he is in a great confusion, as being not only to receive God, but to break and administer him. Neither findes he any issue in this, but to throw himself down at the throne of grace, saying, Lord, thou knowest what thou didst, when thou appointedst it to be done thus; therefore doe thou fulfill what thou didst appoint; for thou art not only the feast, but the way to it" (257). Or again, treating of troubled souls in need of reassurance: "If he sees them neerer desperation, then Atheisme; not so much doubting a God, as that he

The Country Parson

is theirs; then he dives into the boundlesse Ocean of Gods Love, and the unspeakable riches of his loving kindnesse" (283).

The Country Parson, though it is explicitly not autobiographical, tells us a great deal about George Herbert, and for its psychological interest alone it is of great value. It has the additional merit of being delightfully written. Though the plan of the book is not systematic, and it has an unfinished air, within each chapter the discourse proceeds in an orderly and persuasive way. Whether he is writing prose or verse, Herbert never forgets the natural idioms and cadences of spoken English. His phrases are short and to the point, and there is no trace of pomposity in his manner. The parson warns his parishioners "that they dive not too deep into worldly affairs, plunging themselves over head and eares into carking, and caring" (247). Or again, "Those he findes in a peaceable state, he adviseth to be very vigilant, and not to let go the raines as soon as the horse goes easie" (280). But the simplicity of his language is adequate to all demands, like the language of the Book of Common Prayer. When Herbert is treating of a matter that moves him deeply, he conveys his emotion with the minimum of display. Speaking of souls in distress he says: "All may certainly conclude that God loves them, till either they despise that Love, or despaire of his Mercy: not any sin else, but is within his Love: but the despising of Love must needs be without it. The thrusting away of his arme makes us onely not embraced" (283).

Coming to *The Country Parson* with Herbert's poems already in mind, we recognize occasional similarities of phrasing as well as constant similarities of temper. The country parson, for instance, "holds the Rule, that Nothing is little in God's service; if it once have the honour of that Name, it grows great instantly" (249); while the author of *The Elixir* observes:

George Herbert

> All may of thee partake:
> Nothing can be so mean
> That with this tincture (for thy sake)
> Will not grow bright and clean ...
>
> This is the famous stone
> That turneth all to gold,
> For that which God doth touch and own
> Cannot for lesse be told. (p. 184).

The parson who chooses for his sermons texts of "Devotion not Controversie", so seasoning them that his auditors "may plainly perceive that every word is hart-deep" (229) is clearly one with the poet who wrote:

> Could not that Wisdome, which first broacht the wine,
>   Have thicken'd it with definitions?
> And jagg'd his seamlesse coat, had that been fine,
>   With curious questions and divisions?
>
> But all the doctrine, which he taught and gave,
>   Was cleare as heav'n, from whence it came.
> At least those beams of truth, which onely save,
>   Surpasse in brightnesse any flame.
>
> *Love God and love your neighbour. Watch and pray.*
>   *Do as ye would be done unto.*
> O dark instructions; ev'n as dark as day!
>   Who can these Gordian knots undo?
>   (*Divinitie*, p. 134).

In *The Country Parson* there is not a word of the anxieties and feelings of inadequacy which Herbert so often expressed in his poems. There he gave voice to his grief and bewilderment that ill-health and other troubles should thwart him when he had at last dedicated himself to God's service; but

The Country Parson

in *The Country Parson*, the reiterated note is one of joy. "His parish is all his joy and thought" (250); Sunday is his "day of joy" and on Sunday evenings "he thinks it a very fit time, both sutable to the joy of the day, and without hinderance to publick duties, either to entertaine some of his neighbours, or to be entertained of them" (236); "the pulpit is his joy and his throne" (232). Although he writes of "the general ignominy that is cast upon the profession" of a country parson (268), he also says that it is "the greatest honour of this world, to do God and his chosen service" (270).

The atmosphere of tranquillity that pervades *The Country Parson* makes us thankful that George Herbert did not live to see the brief but shattering triumph of the fanatical puritans after the Civil War. At the time when he wrote, though a few dissenters had already broken away to form their own congregations, and the Pilgrim Fathers had established themselves in New England, the majority of puritans still remained officially within the Church of England. They were perpetually voicing their disapproval of her theology, ritual and administration, and arguing about predestination and election; but of this contentious background to the practice of Anglicanism there is scarcely a hint in the reasonable, courteous and quiet disquisitions of *The Country Parson*. The Anglicans as a whole were little exercised by the dogmatic issues raised by Luther and Calvin. They were principally concerned with the Christian faith as a way of life for all, believing that true Christianity was a response, in worship and personal conduct, to God's love as manifested in Christ. "It is a good strife," says Herbert, "to go as farre as wee can in pleasing of him, who hath done so much for us" (224). The characteristic Anglican attitude was a tolerant and temperate one, whether other institutions, or dogmatic difficulties, or human frailties were under consideration, and it was largely because of its

George Herbert

humane temper that Herbert found himself so happily at home in the Church of England. When *The Country Parson* was re-issued after the Restoration, it must have served as a timely reminder of the virtues of that church, so greviously disrupted by the triumph of the dissenters.

V

Herbert's Themes

THERE is a medieval quality about George Herbert's faith that is reflected in his poetry. His wholehearted acceptance of the Church's teaching about God's providence, Man's sin and Christ's redemptive action give him a steady vantage-point from which to contemplate both the world around him and his own inner conflicts. It also determined the character of that contemplation, which was not free, visionary and prophetic, but interpretative.

The orthodox Christian tends to think metaphorically and to work by analogy, since he believes that a divine purpose sustains and informs all things. Consequently he reads religious significance into what he sees or feels, discerning, for instance, the symbol of the resurrection equally in the flowering of a daffodil and in the upspringing of joy in a heart grown accustomed to pain or torpor. How beautifully and naturally Herbert does precisely this can be seen in *The Flower*; and indeed it is his habitual way of commenting on experience.

It is not often that Herbert uses lengthy similes, and when he does (as in *Praise iii*) the result is not very happy; for his was not a rational mind, like Pope's, that easily expatiates on relationships perceived by the intellect. The drawing of parallels fascinated him much less than the discovery of a unifying pattern, linking every form of being in a single, symbolical order. His sonnet *Prayer,* a tissue of metaphors, asserts without the use of a single verb that prayer is a many-sided mystery. The multiple comparisons are all implicit,

George Herbert

because he is primarily seeking a definition by means of analogies; he is not in the least concerned with developing the likenesses that he indicates. Similarly, he does not formally compare himself to a bird in the lines

> In hope of thee my heart
> Pickt here and there a crumme ....
> *(The Glimpse,* p. 154).

nor church music to a bird when he writes:

> Now I in you without a body move,
> Rising and falling with your wings.
> *(Church Musick,* p. 65).

The metaphorical character of his language springs from his constant tendency to co-ordinate and harmonize. He believed whole-heartedly in a supernatural Order that rectifies all discords in the created world; and this intellectual and moral conviction, coupled with his inbred inclination towards sobriety, grace and elegance, accounts for the beautiful orderliness apparent in his poetry.

Herbert's basic assumptions were not in the least idiosyncratic; they were shared by the vast majority of his fellow-countrymen. Although scepticism was in the air, and in the very air that Herbert breathed—his eldest brother paved the way for the advocates of natural religion, Donne was one of those for whom "the new philosophie calls all in doubt"—he himself took for granted the traditional theology and the traditional cosmography that had persisted from pre-reformation times.

> Of what supreme almightie power
> Is thy great arm, which spans the east and west,
>   And tacks the centre to the sphere!
> By it do all things live their measur'd hour;
> We cannot ask the thing, which is not there,
> Blaming the shallownesse of our request.
> *(Prayer,* p. 103).

Herbert's Themes

The universe was still a divinely sustained structure, in which every created thing had its own significance as part of a coherent pattern. The great chain of being, depending from God and linking angels with men, men with beasts and plants and minerals, was one of the generally accepted ideas which Herbert made his own.

> All things are busie: onely I
> Neither bring hony with the bees,
> Nor flowers to make that, nor the husbandrie
> To water these.
>
> I am no link of thy great chain,
> But all my companie is a weed.
> Lord, place me in thy consort; give one strain
> To my poore reed.
>
> (*Employment i*, p. 57).

In these lines we also find the traditional conception of the universe as a divinely organized harmony, an idea specially congenial to the music-loving Herbert. His belief in the essential beauty and goodness of Order colours all his writing. Not only does it find positive verbal expression, as in the long poem *Providence,* but it is expressed in his actual style, so notably coherent, economical and balanced.

The belief that each creature has its proper place and function in a divinely appointed hierarchy is one that can greatly enrich a poet. It fosters a sense of kindship with the whole natural world, from star to stone, saving him from regarding any object as intrinsically mean or any human action as trivial; and it also saves him from what Blake calls "single vision and Newton's sleep". Every phenomenon is a manifestation of God's power and a symbol of his truth.

The interpretative habit of mind, so characteristic of George Herbert, does not necessarily carry with it the visionary gift, though Dante had both. Herbert does not convey, as

George Herbert

Vaughan and Traherne sometimes do, a sudden sense of wonder at half-glimpsed mysteries or veiled glories; but he is continually aware of the implications of what goes on around him. To quote Pascal: "The least movement affects all nature; the entire sea changes because of a rock. Thus in grace, the least action affects everything by its consequences; therefore everything is important."[1]

Man, however, had a unique importance for all who thought as Herbert did. The human constitution reflected, in little, the organization of the cosmos itself. That man was himself a microcosm was a commonplace of medieval thought that survived in full vigour in the seventeenth century, and Herbert often made use of it.

> Man is all symmetrie,
> Full of proportions, one limbe to another,
> And all to all the world besides:
> Each part may call the furthest, brother:
> For head with foot hath private amitie,
> And both with moons and tides.
>
> Nothing hath got so farre,
> But Man hath caught and kept it, as his prey.
> His eyes dismount the highest starre:
> He is in little all the sphere.
>
> *(Man,* p. 91).

Although the angels and celestial powers occupied a higher place in the eternal hierarchy, Man appeared to be the prime beneficiary of the Creator's goodness.

> For us the windes do blowe,
> The earth doth rest, heav'n move, and fountains flow.
> Nothing we see but means our good,
> As our delight, or as our treasure . . .
>
> *(ibid.)*

---

[1] *Pensées,* Everyman's Library, p. 139, (Pensée 505).

Herbert's Themes

Distinguished by his reasoning powers from all the creatures lower in the great chain of being, Man is privileged to be the special recipient of God's bounty because he is capable of appreciating what his true position is, in relation to his Creator.

> Of all the creatures both in sea and land
> Onely to Man thou hast made known thy wayes,
> And put the penne alone into his hand,
> And made him Secretarie of thy praise ...
>
> Man is the worlds high Priest: he doth present
> The sacrifice for all; while they below
> Unto the service mutter an assent,
> Such as springs use that fall, and windes that blow.
>
> *(Providence,* p. 117).

But though Herbert here distinguishes between the kind of thanksgiving that Man and other creatures can render, he often envies the spontaneity with which trees, birds, bees, stars, show forth God's praise by fulfilling the purposes for which they were created.

> Oh that I were an Orenge-tree,
>   That busie plant!
> Then should I ever laden be,
>   And never want
> Some fruit for him that dressed me.
>
> *(Employment ii,* p. 79).

Man's ingratitude is, for Herbert, the strangest and most tragic element in the whole world-picture; for Man's true dignity, as he and other Christian thinkers believed, consists in his being the peculiar focus of God's forgiving love. Man, like the rebel angels, had distorted the original design, brought discord into the original harmony; but God in the person of his Son intervened, to resolve the discords and restore the pattern, by taking upon himself not only the consequences of Man's sin but the very nature of humanity. Because the Son of God became the Son of Man, humanity's position in the cosmological scheme is of unique significance.

Man is capable, as the creatures are not, of entering into a personal relationship with God, a relationship of love. This concept is the very core of Herbert's faith. *The Temple* is, as Professor Grierson observed, a series of metaphysical love poems. "It is a record of God's wooing of the soul of Herbert recorded in the Christian story and the seasons and symbols of the Church, and Herbert's wooing of God, a record of conflict and fluctuating moods, and expostulations with God and himself..."[1] Herbert, however, was not so sentimental as to consider the Divine Love as operating only in the intimate spiritual relationship between God and the individual soul; he also believed that it transcended all personal experience, and was in truth the force upholding the whole scheme of existence.

> We all acknowledge both thy power and love
> To be exact, transcendent and divine;
> Who dost so strongly and so sweetly move,
> While all things have their will, yet none but thine.
>
> *(Providence, p. 117).*

The idea of God's sustaining love pervades Herbert's poetry; but his most frequent and dearest theme is the redemptive love of Christ. He had so thoroughly assimilated the Church's teaching about the atonement that it coloured his entire vision of the world. He realized that the drama of redemption is perpetually being re-enacted, and it is this that gives such poignancy to his poetic treatment of Man's self-will and God's long-suffering.

---

[1] *Cross Currents in English Literature of the 17th Century*, 1929, p. 216.

Herbert's Themes

> Thy life on earth was grief, and thou art still
> Constant unto it, making it to be
> A point of honour, now to grieve in me,
> And in thy members suffer ill.
>   They who lament one crosse,
>   Thou dying dayly, praise thee to thy losse.
>   (*Affliction iii*, p. 73).

The passion of Jesus moved Herbert so profoundly because he was convinced that Man's perversity perpetually wounds the eternal Christ. For the Jews who murdered Jesus he feels an ironic compassion, since he and his fellow-Christians share their guilt. He cannot refer to the sufferings of Christ without a pang of self-reproach; but accompanying the pang comes an upsurge of love.

> I have consider'd it, and finde
> There is no dealing with thy mighty passion:
> For though I die for thee, I am behinde:
> My sinnes deserve the condemnation.
>   (*The Reprisall*, p. 36).

Herbert never speculates on the origin of evil, but Man's propensity to sin constantly oppresses him. From innermost experience he knows how repeatedly even a man convinced of God's love and dedicated to his service will act like an ungrateful, rebellious child.

> could not use a friend, as I use thee.
>   (*Unkindnesse*, p. 93)

Nor does he shrink from considering the magnitude and grievousness of the world's sin, which could be counterbalanced only by the self-sacrificing love of God himself.

George Herbert

> Who would know Sinne, let him repair
> Unto Mount Olivet; there shall he see
> A man so wrung with pains, that all his hair,
>   His skinne, his garments bloudie be.
> Sinne is that presse and vice, which forceth pain
> To hunt his cruell food through every vein.
> (The Agonie, p. 37).

It might be supposed that so tender a poet as Herbert would find special inspiration in the Bethlehem story, but in fact there is only one specifically Christmas poem in *The Temple*. It was the events of Holy Week that stirred his imagination time and again. They are concentrated and presented with astonishing force in *The Sacrifice*, his most powerful poem.

The speaker, as in many medieval poems of a similar type, is Christ on the cross; and all the episodes of his passion, from the agony in the garden to a premonition of the spear piercing his side, are conjured up by the use of the continuous present. The refrain "Was ever grief like mine?" serves to remind us that the Crucified is speaking, and emphasizes the timeless quality of the action; for this is not the tragedy of a good man wronged, but the awful and ironic drama of the giver of all good gifts abused by the takers—the maker of all things flouted by his creatures—almighty God at the mercy of mortal Man. Anyone familiar with the Good Friday Reproaches and with the liturgy of Holy Week must recognize at once that the tone of the poem, that strange blend of compassion and irony, is profoundly traditional. The grandeur of *The Sacrifice* derives from Herbert's complete, unfaltering grasp of the central paradox of Christianity, that the Man of Sorrows is indeed God.

> Then they condemne me all with that same breath,
> Which I do give them daily, unto death.
> Thus *Adam* my first breathing rendereth:
>   Was ever grief like mine? (p. 28).

Herbert's Themes

Again and again the enormity of Man's incomprehension is emphasized, sometimes with a sardonic, sometimes with a tender kind of pity:

> *It is not fit he live a day* they crie,
> Who cannot live lesse than eternally ... (p. 29).

Perhaps the most pregnant verse of the poem is the one that comments on the mockery of the soldiers who crowned Jesus with thorns and hailed him as King:

> Yet since mans scepters are as frail as reeds,
> And thorny all their crowns, bloudie their weeds,
> I, who am Truth, turn into truth their deeds.
>   Was ever grief like mine? (p. 32).

The extreme familiarity of the story, the wealth of ideas traditionally associated with it, and the supremely paradoxical nature of the Christian doctrine concerned, combined to kindle Herbert's poetic imagination to a rare fire; the poem is simultaneously moving and witty, heart-felt and brilliant.[1]

His imaginative grasp of the Christian scheme of salvation was so exceptionally sure that he never had to twist doctrines to suit his own predelictions, as Milton did. The regional idea of Hell, however, is one that he ignored, though he was conscious enough of the hell that alienation from God involves. Heaven was much in his thoughts, but he had too vivid an apprehension of the relationship in this world between

[1] *The Sacrifice* has been minutely analysed by Prof. Rosemond Tuve, in *A Reading of George Herbert*, Faber, 1952. Her essay was provoked by Prof. William Empson's treatment of the poem in *Seven Types of Ambiguity*. Professor Tuve's position is, I think, unassailable; but even with a much smaller amount of critical apparatus, the liturgical and medieval character of *The Sacrifice* can be recognised, and Herbert's debt to the orthodox teachings of the Church fairly assessed.

George Herbert

God and the soul to dwell upon any doctrine of rewards and punishments.

Only two of his poems directly invoke the Holy Spirit, and it is not often that he refers to God as Father, so that his faith appears at first sight strongly Christocentric. In fact, fewer than twenty poems are specifically addressed to Christ. Herbert was too good a Trinitarian to make rigid mental distinctions between the various aspects of the person of God. He calls upon his Lord by a variety of epithets: "Oh, my chief Good!" "Lord of my Soul, love of my minde", "My light, my Feast, my Strength", "Ah, my deare, angrie Lord", "My joy, my life, my crown," sometimes, quite simply, "my deare".

Only a loving study of the New Testament could have engendered this trustful, ardent, childlike approach to God; but Herbert's poems also show at every turn that he knew the Old Testament intimately and valued it dearly. Inevitably, he considered it as historically true as well as divinely inspired; but he read it with poetic understanding, allegorically, in the same way that Spenser and Milton and Blake read the Bible. All were alive to its symbolism and quick to perceive analogies between the Jewish story and human experience, whether recorded or undergone in their own persons. Thus Herbert can write:

> I did towards Canaan draw, but now I am
> Brought back to the Red sea, the sea of shame.
>
> For as the Jews of old, by God's command
>   Travell'd and saw no town;
> So now each Christian hath his journeys spanned:
>   Their storie pennes and sets us down.
> God's works are wide, and let in future times;
> His ancient justice overflows our crimes.
>   (*The Bunch of Grapes*, p. 128).

Herbert's Themes

This way of interpreting the scriptures was, in the seventeenth century, perfectly orthodox. Professor Tuve has illustrated very fully, in *A Reading of George Herbert,* his use of images derived from the Old Testament which, through centuries of employment by the Church, had acquired rich overtones of meaning. Anglicans were still accustomed to associating certain Jewish types with Christian revelations, the Ark prefiguring the Church, the offering of Isaac the gift of God's son and so forth. Some of Herbert's allusions have become obscure to us, thanks to our neglect both of the Bible and of this habit of drawing analogies; but obvious examples of his fondness for the Old Testament can be seen in *Decay, Sion, Aaron* or *Affliction v.*

More imponderable is his debt to the Psalms. In an age when versifiers commonly tried their hands at metrical versions of the psalter, George Herbert has left for posterity only his rendering of the twenty-third psalm, a pleasant though not very remarkable paraphrase. Possibly his constant reading of the psalter, obligatory for a priest, bred in him such a love for the prayer-book words that he did not care to tamper with them. But his daily reading of the psalms as an aid to devotion surely taught him the art of opening his heart to God, no matter what his mood might be. Very many of the psalms are colloquies, in which the soul pleads or remonstrates with God, listens to the divine answer or waits in vain for a response. Such a familiar psalm as the forty-third exemplifies the same rapid, subtle changes of temper that we so often find in the poems of Herbert.

> Give sentence with me, O God, and defend my cause against the ungodly people: O deliver me from the deceitful and wicked man.
> For thou art the God of my strength, why hast thou put me from thee: and why go I so heavily, while the enemy oppresseth me?

George Herbert

> O send out thy light and thy truth that they may lead
> me: and bring me unto thy holy hill, and to thy dwelling.
> And that I may go unto the altar of God, even unto the
> God of my joy and gladness: and upon the harp will I
> give thanks unto thee, O God my God.
> Why art thou so heavy, O my soul: and why art thou so
> disquieted within me?
> O put thy trust in God: for I will yet give him thanks,
> which is the help of my countenance, and my God.

The influence of the psalms upon Herbert's poetry cannot be measured by the accurate notation of echoes, but rather deduced from the ease with which the poet embarks upon a colloquy with his Lord. Herbert's sureness of tone in religious matters is often attributed to his good breeding; his familiarity with the Psalms of David probably had quite as much to do with it. There is, admittedly, no precedent in the psalter for the tenderness, still less for the playfulness, that Herbert sometimes shows in his approaches to God.

> Ah my deare angrie Lord,
> Since thou dost love, yet strike;
> Cast down, yet help afford;
> Sure I will do the like.
>
> I will complain, yet praise;
> I will bewail, approve:
> And all my sowre-sweet dayes
> I will lament, and love.
>
> (*Bitter-sweet.* p. 171).

The willingness to trust God, no matter what befalls, is Hebrew enough, but only a Christian could dare to adopt this tone of voice, or the kind of cajolery that we find in these lines:

Herbert's Themes

> Thou that hast giv'n so much to me,
> Give one thing more, a grateful heart.
> See how thy beggar works on thee
> By art.
> (*Gratefulnesse*, p. 123).

And only a disciplined Christian, like Herbert, could avoid a mawkish overtone of whimsicality when using this tender intonation:—

> Who goeth in the way which Christ hath gone
> Is much more sure to meet with him, then one
> That travelleth by-wayes.
> Perhaps my God, though he be farre before,
> May turn, and take me by the hand, and more
> May strengthen my decayes.
> (*Lent*, p. 87).

The sober good sense of the first three lines counterbalances the wistfulness of the following three in a way that is typical of George Herbert.

The very fact that the patterns of thought, the legends and the symbols which Herbert used were largely traditional throws into higher relief the personality of the poet, when he speaks with his own individual voice. Herbert's sensitiveness to the movements of grace is perhaps the personal quality that emerges most clearly from *The Temple*. His responsiveness to God's goodness is as spontaneous as his shrinking from his harshness; joy and desolation are equally familiar to him. Small wonder that Gerard Manley Hopkins found his love of Herbert "his strongest tie to the English church".[1] No doubt it was disquieting to reflect that this church had not only commanded Herbert's entire loyalty but had also nourished him spiritually into a condition approaching saint-

---

[1] G. F. Lahey, S.J. *Gerard Manley Hopkins*, 1930, p. 19, quoting a remark of Hopkins' friend W. E. Addis.

George Herbert

hood; if a church can breed saints, can it be discredited? Hopkins must have been forcibly struck by the temperamental similarities between himself and Herbert. Both were afflicted by recurrent moods of dejection, when they felt their lives to be futile and unprofitable, and themselves neglected by their Lord and Master. Hopkins'

> cries like dead letters sent
> To dearest him that lives, alas, away [1]

are paralleled by Herbert's unavailing sighs:

> I sent a sigh to seek thee out,
>   Deep drawn in pain,
> Wing'd like an arrow; but my scout
>   Returns in vain.
> *(The Search*, p. 162).

Though Hopkins' cries of anguish are more violent and desperate, Herbert's match them in depth of passion. The quiet conviction of the following lines is as effective testimony to pain endured as any of the tormented laments of Hopkins:

> No scrue, no piercer can
> Into a piece of timber work and winde
>   As God's afflictions into man,
>   When he a torture hath design'd.
> They are too subtill for the subt'llest hearts...
> *(Confession*, p. 126).

Herbert is as baffled as Hopkins by the way in which God often repays loyal service by trials of extreme harshness:

[1] *Poems*, 3rd ed., Oxford, 1948, p. 109.

Herbert's Themes

> Besides, things sort not to my will,
> Ev'n when my will doth studie thy renown:
> Thou turnest th' edge of all things on me still,
>   Taking me up to throw me down:
> So that, ev'n when my hopes seem to be sped,
> I am to grief alive, to them as dead...
>   (*The Crosse*, p. 165).

He is not, however, so heavily oppressed as Hopkins by disgust at himself and his fellow-sinners. In Herbert's poetry his humility often expresses itself in images of childhood or nesting birds; his sense of dependence upon God and his habitual self-distrust come out in such lines as

> O let me still
> Write thee great God, and me a childe:
> Let me be soft and supple to thy will,
>   Small to my self...
>   (*H. Baptisme ii* p. 44).

Because the pain is so unmistakable in a number of the poems, the serenity that Herbert sometimes achieves is the more impressive. It comes not from any facile optimism but from the courageous acceptance of God's will. Acceptance of this kind transcends mere resignation, because it is an affirmative response to a challenge. No poem illustrates this better than *The Temper i*. After lamenting his instability and pleading with God not to try him too hard... "O rack me not to such a vast extent... Will great God measure with a wretch?"... Herbert comes to the supremely simple conclusion:

> Whether I flie with angels, fall with dust,
>   Thy hands made both, and I am there:
> Thy power and love, my love and trust
>   Make one place ev'ry where. (p. 55).

George Herbert

The humility that graces so many of Herbert's poems has nothing in it of creeping submissiveness. Though he often condemns himself for disloyalty to his divine Master, he takes no perverse pleasure in making himself out to be a scoundrel. Sober self-knowledge has brought him, a naturally proud man, to a low estimate of his own worth; but his reliance on God's love is so confident that it overcomes his despondency.

The beauties of Herbert's character are many, and they shine through his writings like light through clear glass. He was not a simple person, though occasionally he seems to us ingenuous. On the contrary, he was a man much torn by inner conflicts, and his poems are primarily, as he himself said, an expression of these tensions. Yet he could sometimes speak with a childlike, lucid simplicity that is the voice of true innocence, the innocence that lies on the far side of experience. William Law defined devotion as "the application of a humble heart to God as its only happiness". This is a yardstick that measures very justly George Herbert's greatness as a devotional poet.

VI

Herbert's Craftsmanship

THE patterns of Herbert's thought and much of the imagery that he used were traditional; but this was no impediment to his originality. Provided that a poet does not simply acquiesce in a creed but grasps it imaginatively, it is a positive advantage to him to have at his command a store of symbols familiar to his contemporaries. He is so much the freer to concentrate upon the formal, structural, technical aspects of his problems. This is what we find with George Herbert. He forged for himself a style that was unmistakable and inimitable; and a poet, after all, is not obliged to invent anything else.

We have evidence in the Williams MS and in the divergences between earlier and later drafts of the same poem[1] that Herbert was a most careful craftsman. Even the slightest of the lyrics in *The Temple* is well-shaped, sinewy and apt. Herbert was a master of economy; where one word will do he does not use more. He seldom strikes off a phrase so brilliant that it lives in isolation, but his poems are wholes; single lines or stanzas suffer when detached from their context, and this is an indication of Herbert's architectonic skill. No poem in *The Temple* is so long that it cannot be rapidly read in its entirety and enjoyed as a well-proportioned structure.

Herbert's poems are full of intellectual vigour. His themes are always serious, sometimes weighty; but he handles them

[1] The revisions made in *The Elixir,* for example, can be profitably studied in F. E. Hutchinson's edition of Herbert's *Works.*

George Herbert

with such skilful grace that the reader follows the poetic logic without difficulty. In many of the "private ejaculations" the movement of the thought corresponds to the development of ideas in conversation or in an interior monologue, except that digressions do not occur. In poems of a more didactic type, the argument is presented lucidly, often symmetrically, so that the reader takes it in his stride, without having to pause (as so often with Donne's poems) to survey the obstacles in his path before being able to surmount them.

Mortification provides a good example of Herbert's more formal method of construction. He passes in review the ages of man, from infancy to senility, in order to show that each stage of existence has its *memento mori*. In every stanza he uses the rhyme-words "breath" and "death", which in themselves are the burden and core of his argument. In *Vanitie* he considers the futility of man's search for knowledge when all thought of God is neglected. He presents his case by citing the astronomer, the diver and the chemist as exemplars of man's desire to explore the universe. Three beautifully balanced stanzas are given to the activities of these searchers, and a fine sense of eagerness is conveyed by the abundant use of verbs that emphasize the different types of investigation:

>   The fleet Astronomer can bore
> And thred the Spheres with his quick-piercing mind:

he runs, walks, surveys, sees and knows; while

>   The subtil Cyhmist can devest
>   And strip the creature naked, till he finde
>   The callow principles ... (p. 85).

The three stanzas, dryly ironic in tone, are capped by the final one in which the pregnant question is put:

>   What hath not man sought out and found,
>   But his deare God?

Herbert's Craftsmanship

The texture of thought and imagery in Herbert's poems is as a rule closely woven, especially in his sonnets. There are fifteen of these in *The Temple*, not counting the two youthful sonnets, published in Walton's *Life*, which he sent to his mother at the outset of his Cambridge career. Herbert probably excluded them from his collected poems because of their slight tinge of priggishness; but as specimens of the sonnet, they are very creditable; the movement is lively, the word-order natural and the conceits apt. Herbert did not experiment with the sonnet form, using always the freest and least Italianate type, with seven rhymes; but he turned it to many uses. There are narrative sonnets, like *Redemption* and *Christmas*; compact arguments, like *The Sinner* or *Joseph's Coat*; *The Holdfast* is a colloquy, *Prayer* a reverie. The two sonnets entitled *Love* are clearly related to the rejected Cambridge sonnets, and their tone calls to mind Spenser, a poet with whom Herbert normally has little in common. Herbert excelled in packing the maximum of meaning into brief compass, and for that reason the sonnet suited him well.

Whatever stanza he chooses, he leaves no loose ends, but brings each poem to a fitting conclusion, sometimes to a brilliantly effective one. The dramatic force of the terse last line of *Redemption* is an example of this:

> At length I heard a ragged noise and mirth
>   Of theeves and murderers: there I him espied
>   Who straight, *Your suit is granted,* said, & died. (p. 40).

The fantastic catalogue of conceits that makes up the sonnet on prayer ends with the profoundly simple phrase, "something understood". *The Collar, Affliction i, Miserie, Thanksgiving,* are some of the poems which end with a sudden and most dramatic change of mood.

George Herbert

His openings are equally well contrived. The attention is immediately caught by such lines as

> Busie enquiring heart, what wouldst thou know?

or

> Meeting with Time, Slack thing, said I,

or

> Kill me not every day.

Sometimes the verses of a poem are made interdependent by the use of repetitive imagery. In *Ungratefulnesse,* for instance, cabinets and boxes figure in all but the last stanza; in *Obedience,* legal phrases are employed in all but two of the seven verses. Alternatively Herbert may use a refrain to bind his verses one to another; or he may restrict himself to a few repeated rhymes, as in *Aaron,* where the five words, head, breast, dead, rest, drest, are the rhyme-words in every one of the five stanzas, and their order is never varied; or as in *Clasping of Hands,* where a poem of twenty lines has only the four rhyming words, thine, mine, more, restore. It would be tedious to multiply examples of the devices which Herbert uses to make each poem a shapely and telling unit. No careful reader of *The Temple* can fail to be impressed by his good workmanship.

Herbert's conscious striving to achieve a style wholly free from affectation is expressed in the two *Jordan* poems, in *The Forerunners* and *A True Hymne.* It was not a merely literary pursuit, dictated by critical preference for a plain rather than an embellished style. It was an integral part of his moral struggle to achieve sincerity. His poetry, like his life, was dedicated to God, and for that reason it had to be disciplined and divested of "fictions... and false hair". There is plenty of evidence that elaboration attracted him. In *Dulnesse,* he openly envies the artifice of worldlier poets:

Herbert's Craftsmanship

> The wanton lover in a curious strain
>   Can praise his fairest fair;
> And with quaint metaphors her curled hair
>   Curl o're again . . .
>
> Where are my lines, then? my approaches? views?
>   Where are my window-songs? . . . (p. 115).

The sheer pleasure afforded by ingenuity accounts for poems like *A Wreath, Easter Wings* or *Paradise*; and Herbert was reluctant to give up this pleasure. Towards the end of his life, as ill-health wore him down, it would appear that his eloquence and verbal dexterity began at times to fail him; and he was grieved by this inability to express himself fluently. In *The Forerunners* he speaks of the white hairs that have appeared to warn him of approaching old age, and he laments that his mental powers too should be threatened with loss of brilliance. His brain no longer breeds "those sparkling notions", and he cries:

> Farewell, sweet phrases, lovely metaphors . . .
>
> Lovely, enchanting language, sugar-cane,
> Hony of roses, whither wilt thou flie? (p. 176).

This is the utterance of a man who indeed relished versing, and had a truly Elizabethan joy in the play and resources of the English language.

> I like our language, as our men and coast.
> Who cannot dresse it well, want wit, not words.
>   (*The Sonne*, p. 167).

The Sidneian element in Herbert has been underestimated, because of the biographical link with Donne and the consequent critical assumption that he was strongly affected by the metaphysical fashion in poetry. We have only to compare George Herbert's poems with those of his eldest brother to see how independent he kept himself from any literary vogue. Lord Herbert's natural bent for metaphysics in the strict sense of the word naturally inclined him to outmatch Donne by loading his poems with a profusion of learned allusions and philosophical terms. George Herbert was familiar with the new line of wit, and sometimes he followed it; but an outstanding characteristic of his verse is its beautiful flexibility and singing quality. These are pre-eminently the merits of the Elizabethan song-writers. Campion and his fellows, writing for the voice, had evolved stanzas of extraordinary fluency which yet kept the natural rhythms of spoken English. Herbert's variety of stanza form is quite exceptional. So, in his period, is his frequent use of refrain and of various musician-like devices, common enough among lutenists from Wyatt onwards.

From Herbert's poetry we could deduce what Walton tells us, that music was, outside religion, his greatest joy. Not only are the allusions to music very numerous, but many of the poems are constructed with a sense of form that is in itself musicianly. Sometimes this is done almost too deliberately, as in *Sinnes Round*. Here the punning title gives a clue to the form. The concluding line of each stanza is repeated as the opening line of the next, and the last line of the poem is identical with the first, so that the sense comes full circle, and the movement is like that of a musical round. It is, however, highly appropriate to its subject, for the continual repetition of sin is the precise point that Herbert wants to make.

In *Home*, a lengthy poem of longing to be quit of "this world of wo", he produces exactly the effect of a modulation of key. The two concluding verses run:

Herbert's Craftsmanship

>What have I left, that I should stay and grone?
> The most of me to heav'n is fled:
>My thoughts and joyes are all packt up and gone,
> And for their old acquaintance plead.
>   O show thyself to me,
>   Or take me up to thee!
>
>Come, dearest Lord, passe not this holy season,
> My flesh and bones and joynts do pray:
>And ev'n my verse, when by the ryme and reason,
> The word is *Stay*, says ever, *Come*.
>   O show thyself to me,
>   Or take me up to thee! (p. 109).

Not only does the substitution of "Come" for the rhyme-word "Stay" effect a key-change, it adds point to the title of the poem, in which the missing rhyme for "Come" is to be found. In *Deniall* the change of key at the end is brought about by the reverse process. Whereas the final rhyme of each stanza has been wanting, in the last stanza it is supplied, so that the minor modulates to the major. To quote the last two verses:

>Therefore my soul lay out of sight,
> Untun'd, unstrung:
>My feeble spirit, unable to look right.
> Like a nip't blossome, hung
>   Discontented.
>
>O cheer and tune my heartlesse breast,
> Defer no time;
>That so thy favours granting my request,
> They and my minde may chime,
>   And mend my ryme. (p. 80).

A number of poems in *The Temple* were clearly written to be sung. Some are suitable for singing in church and

George Herbert

have in the course of time been included in hymn-books; others are intended for singing to the lute. *Easter*, for instance, is as well and as consciously adapted for a musical setting as any piece by Campion.

As regards the great variety of stanza-forms used by Herbert, his editor G. H. Palmer remarks that of the 169 poems in *The Temple*, 116 are written in metres that are not repeated; for Herbert "invents for each lyrical situation exactly the rhythmic setting that befits it".[1] Any number of examples can be adduced to prove this point. To match the headstrong mood of *The Collar*, we have an unparagraphed run of free (though rhyming) verse; for *Submission* a rather meek-sounding quatrain is chosen. The principle that the dominant emotion of each poem dictates its rhythmic form runs right through the book. It is perhaps worth remarking that Herbert makes no use of the octosyllabic couplet, so beautifully used by his contemporary Henry King, and later by Marvell and Milton; nor does he employ the lovely stanza that his brother Edward used several times with great success, which Tennyson adopted for *In Memoriam*.

Herbert may have learnt a good deal from Donne about the possibilities of varying stanza-forms, for Donne too is inventive in this respect; but whereas his verse struck some of his contemporaries as harsh and rhythmically unpleasant, Herbert's, though energetic, is never dissonant. His poems are all fashioned with a musician's attention to beauty of cadence.

Since he chose to cast so many of his poems in the form of colloquies, either with God or with his own heart, Herbert naturally employed with great freedom the phrases and rhythms of actual speech. The remarkable thing is that he managed to combine these colloquial rhythms with such elegant stanza-forms and rhyme-schemes. His verse is much

---

[1] *English Works of George Herbert*, 3 vols., 2nd ed. 1915, Houghton Mifflin. Vol., I, p. 135.

Herbert's Craftsmanship

more dramatic in effect than any of the Elizabethan song-writers' lyrics, for it is constantly enlivened with questions, exclamations and admonitions. Occasionally, as in *Love Unknown,* Herbert writes dialogue. This particular poem, with its many parentheses, its slowly developing narrative and the comments interjected by the second speaker, suggests that he could have turned his hand to dramatic verse if he had cared to do so. Often snatches of conversation are incorporated in the poems, as in *The Quip* or *Peace.* Herbert's favourite form, however, is the one-sided conversation. If he is addressing his conscience, or an unruly thought, or his recalcitrant heart, he will vary his tone, sometimes upbraiding, sometimes challenging. He makes his unsubstantial foes thoroughly human, investing them with bodies that can be seated or clad, even throats that can be choked:

>   Now foolish thought go on,
>   Spin out thy thread, and make thereof a coat
>   To hide thy shame: for thou hast cast a bone
>   Which bounds on thee, and will not down thy throat:
>   (*Assurance,* p. 156).

or again:

>   Content thee, greedie heart ...
>
>   To be in both worlds full
>   Is more then God was, who was hungrie here.
>   Wouldst thou his laws of fasting disannull?
>   Enact good cheer?
>   Lay out thy joy, yet hope to save it?
>   Wouldst thou both eat thy cake, and have it? ...
>
>   Wherefore sit down, good heart;
>   Grasp not at much, for fear thou losest all ...
>   (*The Size,* p. 138).

George Herbert

The stanza quoted above is a good example of Herbert's fondness for proverbs and for a battery of questions. The first two verses of *Jordon i* are an unbroken series of questions. *Discharge* opens with two stanzas of questions, followed by four of admonition; then come three of general reflection, and the last two are again admonitory. Some twenty poems in *The Temple* begin with a question, and there are few in which Herbert does not use the interrogative. The opening of *The Glimpse* illustrates his skill in conveying the very cadences of the speaking voice; a reiteration of plaintive questions is followed by two reflective, half-humorous lines, as though he had added them in an undertone:

> Whither away delight?
> Thou cam'st but now; wilt thou so soon depart,
>   And give me up to night?
> For many weeks of lingring pain and smart
> But one half houre of comfort to my heart?
>
> Me thinks delight should have
> More skill in musick, and keep better time... (p. 154).

Though Herbert's language is normally colloquial, it can rise to occasional grandeur. We have only to compare his two very dissimilar treatments of the same image, one in *The Church-floore,* the other in *Church Monuments,* to perceive the variety of which he was capable. The first is characteristically domestic:

> Sometimes Death, puffing at the doore,
>   Blows all the dust about the floore;
>   But while he thinks to spoil the room, he sweeps. (p. 67).

The second invests Death's outbreathings with solemn terror:

Herbert's Craftsmanship

>   While that my soul repairs to her devotion,
>   Here I intombe my flesh, that it betimes
>   May take acquaintance of this heap of dust;
>   To which the blast of deaths incessant motion,
>   Fed with the exhalation of our crimes,
>   Drives all at last ... (p. 64).

But Herbert very rarely writes with sustained magnificence, as he does throughout the entire poem from which these lines are taken. Coleridge's estimate of his diction is essentially perceptive and just: "nothing can be more pure, manly and unaffected".

His familiarity with country people as well as with those of the university and the court ensured that his language was free from preciousness. The proportion of rustic words in his vocabulary is not at all high, but when they do occur they take their place appropriately in phrases that are simple and energetic. Three successive verses from *Content* will serve to illustrate Herbert's style at its most countrified:

>   The brags of life are but a nine days wonder;
>   And after death the fumes that spring
>   From private bodies make as big a thunder
>   As those which rise from a huge King.
>
>   Onely thy Chronicle is lost; and yet
>   Better by worms be all once spent,
>   Then to have hellish moths still gnaw and fret
>   Thy name in books, which may not rent:
>
>   When all thy deeds, whose brunt thou feel'st alone,
>   Are chaw'd by others pens and tongue;
>   And as their wit is, their digestion,
>   Thy nourisht fame is weak or strong. (p. 69).

Herbert's fondness for drawing his comparisons from episodes and objects of everyday life has been remarked by every critic, whether, as in the eighteenth century, in deprecation, or, as at present, in commendation. It scarcely needs illustration. Of anxiety, Herbert writes

> God chains the dog till night; wilt loose the chain
> And wake thy sorrow? ...
>
> (*The Discharge* p. 145).

God is compared to an angler:

> Thy double line
> And sev'rall baits in either kinde
> Furnish thy table to thy minde.
>
> (*Affliction v*, p. 97).

Of his misgivings, he observes

> My thoughts are all a case of knives. (*Affliction iv*, p. 90).

Many of his images and conceits, as Professor Tuve has amply illustrated, are not so far-fetched as they at first sight appear. A very large proportion are of biblical origin, and were not unfamiliar to people educated in the tradition of drawing parallels between scriptural incidents and church doctrines. Solomon's sea of brass, or Justice's balance of which

> The beam and scrape
> Did like some torturing engine show
>
> (*Justice ii*, p. 141).

were more easily comprehensible to Herbert's readers than to the average reader today.

The vitality of his conceits derives rather from the play of his lively, sensitive mind upon familiar and consecrated material than from brilliance of invention or daringness in juxtaposition. Sometimes his fancy leads him to embody a

Herbert's Craftsmanship

conceit in the title of his poem; there is no actual mention of a pulley or of a collar in the poems that go by these names. Often Herbert is content to indicate the analogy he wishes to make, and to leave it at that.

There are, however, poems in which he uses images in much the same way as did the compilers of Emblem Books. Miss Freeman makes some excellent points in her chapter on Herbert,[1] though she overstates her case when she maintains that "It cannot be too strongly emphasized that Herbert's images remain emblems and at no time encroach upon the wider province of the symbol. There is no necessary resemblance between the church floor and the human heart, between stained-glass windows and preachers, or between two cabinets containing treasure and the Trinity and the Incarnation. His method is always to create meanings by creating likenesses; the likenesses are rarely inherent in the imagery chosen, nor can they often be seen from the outset".[2] Although there are several poems in *The Temple* which perfectly illustrate "a readiness to see a relation between simple, concrete, visible things and moral ideas, and to establish that relation in as complete a way as possible without identifying the two or blurring the outline of either",[3] there are many more that testify to the far rarer gift that Herbert possessed, of being able to discern the divine order in everyday experience, and to perceive, rather than establish, relations between the visible and the spiritual.

Surely Herbert's sustained use of imagery in *The Flower* shows an exquisite control of the symbolism of winter and desolation, spring and hope renewed, the garden and paradise. In *The Priesthood* he employs the image of the potter's clay in

---

[1] *English Emblem Books*, Chatto & Windus, 1948.

[2] *op. cit* p. 163.

[3] *op. cit.* p. 155.

consecutive stanzas, varying its significance, but never in an arbitrary way. It is a valid symbol at once of man's creaturely inferiority and of his malleability in the hands of God. There is nothing "emblematic" in the use of the ancient symbols of rock and storm in this stanza from *Assurance*:

> Wherefore if thou canst fail,
> Then can thy truth and I: but while rocks stand,
> And rivers stirre, thou canst not shrink or quail:
> Yea, when both rocks and all things shall disband,
>   Then shalt thou be my rock and tower,
>   And make their ruine praise thy power. (p. 156).

Or again, to illustrate the rapidity with which Herbert sometimes shifts his imagery (not an "emblematic" trait), we may take the opening lines of *The Answer*:

> My comforts drop and melt away like snow:
> I shake my head, and all the thoughts and ends,
> Which my fierce youth did bandie, fall and flow
> Like leaves about me: or like summer friends,
> Flyes of estates and sunne-shine . . . (p. 169).

Miss Freeman also contends that "Herbert's poetry brings its pictures with it. It remains primarily visual, but the images presented have already been explored and when they enter the poem they enter it with their implications already worked out".[1] Well-defined his images certainly are; but not markedly pictorial. There are very few colours mentioned in Herbert's poems, although the symbolism of light is constantly used. Even when we might legitimately expect description, we do not get it. The first verse of *The Pilgrimage*, for instance, could scarcely be starker:

[1] *op. cit.* p. 155.

Herbert's Craftsmanship

> I travell'd on, seeing the hill, where lay
>   My expectation.
> A long it was and weary way.
> The gloomy cave of Desperation
> I left on th'one, and on the other side
>   The rock of Pride. (p. 141).

If we imagine for a moment what Spenser would have made of this material, it seems scarcely just to describe Herbert as a visual poet. Similarly, when he personifies Obedience, only her attitude is conveyed, not her visible attributes:

> Humble Obedience neare the doore doth stand,
>   Expecting a command:
> Then whom in waiting nothing seems more slow,
>   Nothing more quick when she doth goe.
>   (*The Familie*, p. 137).

Herbert makes his verbs work harder than his adjectives. This is one of the essential features of his energetic, masculine style, but it does not make for pictorial effects. Writing of afflictions, he uses an unexpected simile, the force of which depends chiefly upon the succession of words expressing action:

> We are the earth; and they
> Like moles within us, heave, and cast about,
> And till they foot and clutch their prey,
> They never cool, much lesse give out.
>   (*Confession*, p. 126).

But if Herbert's visual sensibility was not remarkable, we may deduce from his imagery that his sense of smell and taste was very acute, for his customary way of expressing moods of ecstasy is by reference to perfumes and delicious sweetness. *The Odour* and *The Banquet* are obvious examples, but there are plenty of others scattered throughout *The Temple*:

> I felt a sugred strange delight,
> Passing all cordials made by any art,
> Bedew, embalme, and overrunne my heart...
> (*The Glance*, p. 171).

> What though some have a fraught
> Of cloves and nutmegs, and in cinamon sail;
> If thou hast wherewithall to spice a draught,
>   When griefs prevail;
> And for the future time art heir
> To th' Isle of spices, is't not fair?
> (*The Size*, p. 137).

> Lovely enchanting language, sugar-cane,
> Hony of roses, whither wilt thou flie?
> (*The Forerunners*, p. 176).

These, and similar passages, testify to Herbert's protest, "My stuffe is flesh, not brasse; my senses live". Of all his sense-allusions, perhaps the simplest and most sensitive of all is the line from *The Flower*

> I once more smell the dew and rain,

where these few words convey the essence of the joy that accompanies the cessation of spiritual aridity.

Musical analogies, as we should expect, are very numerous in Herbert's verse, and so, not surprisingly, are sick-room metaphors. A great many images are derived from the domestic background of house and garden. To illustrate

Herbert's Craftmanship

these would be wearisome; they leap to the eye of even the cursory reader.

Herbert's sheer enjoyment of metaphor comes out in the first two stanzas of *Dotage*, where the pleasures and sorrows of life are summed up and contrasted in a long series of juxtaposed images. The same thing can be seen even more vividly in *Prayer i*, a poem that contains not a single direct statement, but consists entirely of brief analogies that combine to throw light on the mystery that is the poet's theme.

Usually Herbert's imagery is unobtrusive. He seldom labours his points; indeed, his jests are sometimes so quiet that they almost escape notice, as in the lines

> Who sweeps a room as for thy laws
> Makes that and th' action fine.
> *(The Elixir*, p. 184).

He can occasionally be grotesque:

> Death, thou wast once an uncouth, hideous thing,
> Nothing but bones,
> The sad effect of sadder grones;
> Thy mouth was open, but thou couldst not sing.
> *(Death*, p. 185).

Very rarely does he let his fancy play around an abstract notion, though he does so in *Sinne ii*, which is the amplification of a scholastic quibble. It is in every sense of the word a metaphysical poem, and not a distinguished one. It would not have disgraced Edward Herbert, but it is quite untypical of his brother.

As a rule George Herbert's conceits blend into the general texture of his verse. The whole mattered to him more than the parts, and his desire to co-ordinate generally prevented him from embroidering any one conceit so elaborately that it would draw attention to itself and away from the gist of the poem as a whole. A sense of proportion and balance characterized his thinking and also his poetic workmanship.

We might almost deduce from his writings, if we did not know it from the record of his life, that Herbert was an accomplished speaker. He manages his rhythms and diction as though he were actually expending his breath. There are no strident forcings of the voice, no lapses into colourless undertone. He knows the range of the instrument at his command and uses all its resources with discrimination and skill. Practitioners of verse can learn much from a study of *The Temple*.

VII

Literary Affinities

AFTER an examination of Herbert's poetic workmanship we are in a better position to assess his debt to Donne; and there are many reasons for concluding that this indebtedness has been exaggerated. Let it be acknowledged immediately that Herbert's poetry resembles Donne's in its blend of vigorous thought with subtle emotion; the "tough reasonableness beneath the lyric grace" is as discernible in the one as in the other, and Donne was the pioneer in this kind of writing. His example may also have influenced the younger man to dedicate his poetic gifts to sacred themes. There are, moreover, poems in *The Temple* which remind us that Herbert, through his mother, enjoyed exceptional opportunities of studying Donne's unpublished verse.[1] The "parody" of *Soul's Joy* comes at once to mind, and *Church Monuments*, with its sombre imagery and unusually impressive diction; the resemblance between *The Church Militant*, a poem quite untypical of Herbert, and Donne's Satires has also been mentioned. There are, besides, a certain number of similarities in phraseology that could be picked out. Nevertheless, the total effect of Herbert's style is so unlike Donne's, and his avowed intention so different, that we must give him credit for reading the older poet's verses critically. A man of his intelligence must have perceived from the outset the temperamental differences between himself and Donne, and the

[1] Donne's *Poems* first appeared two years after his death, in 1633, the year in which *The Temple* was also published.

consequent unsuitability of taking him as a master in poetic method.

Had Herbert wished to do so, he could have loaded his poetry with recondite allusions. Though he clearly felt the impact of the new learning much less than Donne, he moved in the circles most concerned with it; and he was, besides, a distinguished student of the classics, of divinity and of the art of rhetoric. In spite of this he took pains to avoid all display of erudition in his writings. Nor did he, like Donne, pursue an idea or an image through tortuous verse-paragraphs, nor allow subtlety of thought to impose harshness on his phrasing. If the vigour of his language reminds us of Donne, he had other exemplars too, notably Raleigh and Sidney; and among his contemporaries Ben Jonson, to whom the label "metaphysical" is not accorded, could be equally energetic and forthright.

When Jonson writes:

> And this Securitie
> It is the common Moath
> That eats on Wits and Arts, and destroys them both [1]

it might be Herbert, except for the uneven movement of the last line; and there is a strong resemblance in tone as well as in vigour of language between several stanzas of *Miserie* and Ben Jonson's *Ode to Himself* from *The New Inne*. Jonson was a fervent admirer of Edward Herbert, but besides writing an elegy in *Underwoods* in Lord Herbert's favourite type of quatrain, he printed there a few devotional poems remarkably close in style and feeling to George Herbert's. He must have been moved to write *A Hymn to God the Father* by a reading of *The Temple* as a whole, for it is not one specific poem that he imitates; rather, it is the simple, direct spirit and diction so

[1] *Poems,* ed. B. H. Newdigate, 1936, p. 124.

Literary Affinities

characteristic of Herbert, and so uncharacteristic of Donne. The first three verses of Jonson's *Hymn* will serve to prove this point:

> Heare mee, O God!
> A broken heart
> Is my best part:
> Use still thy rod,
> That I may prove
> Therein, thy Love.
>
> If thou hadst not
> Been sterne to mee,
> But left me free,
> I had forgot
> My selfe and thee.
>
> For, sin's so sweet,
> As minds ill bent
> Rarely repent,
> Untill they meet
> Their punishment.[1]

Besides bringing Herbert to mind, these lines recall Wyatt; and if a literary genealogy must be traced for Herbert, there is much to be said for affiliating him to Wyatt and Sidney as well as to Donne.

There are biographical as well as literary reasons for linking Herbert with Sidney. The families were connected by the marriage of Mary Sidney, Sir Philip's renowned sister, herself a poet, with Henry Herbert, Earl of Pembroke.[2] It was the

---

[1] *op. cit.* p. 87.

[2] There was another connection, much more remote, but not without interest. The eldest brother of Sir John Danvers, Herbert's step-father, had been page to Sir Philip Sidney.

George Herbert

sons of this marriage, William and Philip, who were responsible for introducing their kinsman George to King James, and later for presenting him with the living of Bemerton. But long before the poet came to live in the neighbourhood of Wilton, the birthplace of *Arcadia,* he seems to have held the writings of Sidney in high regard.

Magdalen Herbert, with seven sons to bring up, cannot have failed to set before them the example of their illustrious kinsman, who was the very pattern of Christian chivalry to his countrymen. An indication of George's familiarity with Sidney's poetic ideals can be found in the two sonnets which he sent, with a covering letter, as a new year's gift to his mother when he was a seventeen-year-old freshman at Trinity College, Cambridge. The first sonnet asks, in a series of passionate questions, why poets do not use their gifts to glorify God:

>   Doth Poetry
> Weare *Venus* Livery? onely serve her turn?
> Why are not *Sonnets* made of thee? and layes
>   Upon thine Altar burnt?   Cannot thy love
>   Heighten a spirit to sound out thy praise
> As well as any she?   (p. 206).

The second sonnet answers the questions with the affirmation that God is infinitely better worth praising than mortal beauty, which is corruptible:

> Open the bones, and you shall nothing find
>   In the best *face,* but *filth,* when, Lord, in thee
>   The *beauty* lies in the *discovery.*

In the accompanying letter he wrote: "For my own part, my meaning (*dear Mother*) is in these Sonnets, to declare my resolution to be, that my poor Abilities in *Poetry,* shall be all,

Literary Affinities

and ever consecrated to God's glory" (p. 363). This resolution, in spite of worldly ambitions and distractions, he never broke; and he may have been impelled towards taking it by the consideration of a passage in Sidney's *Apology for Poetry* :—

"Other sorts of Poetry almost have we none, but that lyrical kind of songs and sonnets; which, Lord, if He gave us so good minds, how well it might be employed, and with how heavenly fruit, both private and public, in singing the praises of the immortal beauty, the immortal goodness of that God Who giveth us hands to write and wits to conceive; of which we might well want words, but never matter; of which we could turn our eyes to nothing, but we should ever have new budding occasions."[1]

Besides this, Sidney left a more intimate testimony in the last two sonnets printed in the *Arcadia* volume; poems that express his sense of the waste of time and energy which he had spent in the pursuit of mortal love and the celebration of mortal beauty. In one sonnet he laments:

    Desire! Desire! I have too dearly bought
    With prise of mangled mind, thy worthless ware:[2]

in the other, he renounces earthly love in favour of heavenly:

    Leave me, O Love, that reachest but to dust;
    And thou, my mind, aspire to higher things . . .[3]

Besides these precepts of Sidney, Herbert had before him the actual example of Donne, whose Divine Poems were inflamed by as ardent a passion as the love poetry he had abandoned. Herbert's critical affinities with Sidney come out most clearly when we compare their views on the writing of

[1] *English Critical Essays of the xvi–xvii Centuries,* World's Classics, p. 58.
[2] and [3] *Poems,* ed. Grosart, 1877, vol. I, p. 147.

verse. There is remarkable agreement between the two poets on the need for authenticity of experience and simplicity of expression.

In several sonnets of the *Astrophel to Stella* sequence, Sidney dissociates himself from the writers of merely complimentary verses, who eke out their want of matter with ingenious figures and elegancies borrowed from abroad. "Pindar's apes," he calls them, and boasts, "I am no pick-purse of another's wit." He reproves

> You that poore Petrarch's long-deceased woes
> With new-borne sighs and denisen'd wit do sing;
> You take wrong wayes; those far-fet helps be such
> As do bewray a want of inward tuch,
> And sure, at length stolne goods doe come to light.[1]

He admits that in the past he has himself been guilty of just such practices, but claims that he now has an authentic experience to draw on, authentic feelings to express, and that consequently he realizes the folly and falsity of this kind of versifying. His assertion is not substantiated by his practice, for there is a great deal of borrowed material in the *Astrophel* sequence; but he does emphatically proclaim the superiority, in love poetry, of simple sincerity to affected hyperbole. The opening sonnet of the sequence purports to set the key for the whole series, and it affords a curiously close parallel to Herbert's second *Jordan* poem (originally entitled *Invention*) in which he recounts his own development as a poet.

Sidney in this sonnet and Herbert in *Jordan ii* both say that the wish to create something arresting led them astray. The elaboration of style that they proposed to themselves distracted their attention from the genuine feelings which had in the first place impelled them to write. Both resolve the

[1] *op. cit.* p. 25.

dilemma in the same way, by returning to essentials. *Foole, said my Muse to me, looke in thy heart, and write.* This is Sidney's conclusion, and Herbert's is similar:

> How wide is all this long pretence!
> There is in love a sweetnesse readie penn'd.
> Copie out onely that, and save expense.   (p. 103).

Herbert, writing religious poetry, was perpetually on his guard against insincerity. The extravagance that in secular love-lyrics may be merely a fault of taste is more seriously damaging to devotional verse, which is addressed to God, "to whom all hearts are open, and from whom no secrets are hid". In *Jordan i* he abruptly questions the merits of highly-wrought verse, and asserts the superiority, for his own purposes, of a sober and simple style; and this poem also calls to mind Sidney, who protested "I do not envy Aristotle's wit" and, contrasting himself with magniloquent lovers, claimed, "I can speake what I feele, and feele as much as they".

Their love of what is heart-felt and forthright is one of the great bonds between these two poets. Sidney was capable of writing in an exquisitely simple style that must have been more congenial to Herbert (to judge by what he himself tells us of his tastes) than the often tortuous convolutions of Donne. Some of his songs are almost monosyllabic, yet most beautifully cadenced; and in the sonnets there are lines which reach the extreme heights of simplicity—heights which Herbert too could scale. Speaking of his passion for Stella, Sidney says:

> And Love doth hold my hand, and makes me write.[1]

This is echoed by Herbert in *Assurance*:

> Thou didst at once thy self indite,
> And hold my hand, while I did write.   (p. 156).

[1] *op. cit.* p. 118.

George Herbert

and it is more subtly re-echoed in the lines

> Love took my hand, and smiling did reply,
> Who made the eyes but I?
>
> *(Love iii, p. 189).*

When Herbert wrote the wonderful conclusion of *Affliction i*

> Ah, my deare Lord, though I be clean forgot,
> Let me not love thee, if I love thee not.

he was almost writing a variation on Sidney's line

> Deare, love me not, that you may love me more.[1]

There is also a vein of neo-platonic thought in Herbert, notably in the two sonnets *Immortal Love* and *Immortal Heat*, which connects him with Sidney; but perhaps enough has been said to suggest that Donne's was not the only major influence in the shaping of Herbert's poetic style.

It is worth remembering, too, that he only outlived by a very few years the great lutenist writers, Dowland and Campion. There is much in Herbert's poetry that connects it with the golden age of song.

The quality which Herbert has in common with Donne is the ability to apply his whole intelligence, reason and sensibility simultaneously, to whatever experience he is shaping into a poem. If it was due to his study of Donne that Herbert was able so to exercise his powers, then his debt was certainly great; but it remains very general. He felt the stimulus, but he did not succumb, as his brother Edward did, to the seduction of Donne's poetic methods.

There can be no question of the propriety of calling Lord Herbert of Cherbury a metaphysical poet, whichever of the

---

[1] *op. cit.* p. 84.

Literary Affinities

varying definitions of that tiresome term be adopted. He was undoubtedly an admirer of Donne; his verse abounds in learned allusions and odd analogies; its prevailing temper is restless and speculative; and he was perpetually preoccupied with metaphysical problems.

Edward Herbert cannot write a madrigal without employing philosopher's terms:

> You, universal beauty seem to me,
> Giving and shewing form and degree
> To all the rest.[1]

Of a rosebud he writes:

> ... a budding Rose, when first 'tis blown,
> Smells sweeter far, then when it is more spread,
> As all things best by principles are known:[2]

The sight of a wax candle burning out moves him to a highly typical piece of speculation. He addresses the candle as though it were a sentient being:

> Thou still do'st grow more short of thy desire
> And do'st in vain unto that place aspire,
> To which thy native powers seem inclin'd.[3]

Reflecting that the dissolution of the candle consigns the material part to ashes, the light to "higher regions", he concludes that nothing is wasted:

> Some parts of thee make up this Universe,
> Others a kind of dignity obtain ...
> Much more our Souls then ...

[1] *Poems*, ed. G. C. Moore Smith, Oxford, 1923, p. 18.
[2] p. 67.
[3] p. 83.

George Herbert

Here is the true extended metaphysical conceit, for he goes on to consider that our "poor Carkasses" will be resolved into their elements and may be re-activated—"Quicken'd again by the world's common soul". This is no evil fate for our bodies; and how much more hopeful is the outlook for the soul, "our part divine", which can expect, like the candle's light, to be reassumed into the divinity from which it originated. Other good and highly metaphysical poems are the sonnet *To Black it self* and *To his Watch when he could not sleep*.

The argumentative progression of thought, that gives sinew to all metaphysical poetry, becomes pedantically logical at times in Lord Herbert's verse. Even his masterpiece, the *Ode on a Question moved, whether Love should continue for ever* suffers when compared with Donne's *The Ecstasie,* largely because the argument is conducted in a more detached and scholastic manner. Many of his poems, too, suffer from his inability to resist intellectual acrobatics. Too often the conceits in Edward Herbert's verse remain merely cerebral; ideas intrigued him, but he did not always wait until a kindling emotion gave them poetic validity. When there is genuine fusion of thought and feeling, as there is in the *Ode,* or in the *Elegy over a Tomb,* he can write magnificently.

Throughout his poetry, in marked contrast with that of his brother George, we find conceits drawn from philosophy, geometry, alchemy, physics and other fields of learning; and more often than not, these conceits are relentlessly worked out, as though to prove the writer's competence as a logician. The last verse of *The First Meeting* will serve as an example:

> Only as we in Loadstones find
>   Vertue of such a kind,
>   That what they once do give
> B'ing neither to be chang'd by any Clime,
>   Or forc'd by time,

> Doth ever in its subjects live;
> So though I be from you retir'd,
>   The power you gave yet still abides,
>   And my soul ever so guides,
> By your magnetique touch inspir'd,
> That all it moves, or is inclin'd,
> Comes from the motion of your mind.[1]

The words "prove" and "define" occur with significant frequency in Lord Herbert's verse, whereas we very seldom find in his brother's writings echoes of scholastic logic-chopping. There are among George Herbert's poems a few in which he uses the extended conceit; *The Odour* is one, *Grief* another; but even though these poems have the fancifulness that is characteristic of verse written in the Donne tradition, they are not syllogistic in structure, but are energized more by emotion than reason.

The poetry of Lord Herbert differs so radically from that of his brother that one may ask whether, if the one is appropriately described as a metaphysical poet, the other should be labelled with the same tag. A cap that fits the one will not fit the other, unless it is twisted into an unrecognizable shape.[2]

The one quality which they have in common is wit; that ability, by a co-ordinated movement of mind and heart, to express unexpected analogies and surprise the reader into intelligent attention. This wit is presumably called metaphysical because it so often connects the abstract with the concrete; but impulses to draw analogies between the near and the far may arise from two quite different habits of mind.

A sceptical and scientific attitude, or a medievally complete

---

[1] *op. cit.* p. 41.

[2] Harold E. Hutcheson, in the introduction to his edition of Lord Herbert's *De Religione Laici* (Yale, 1944), considers it misleading to associate George Herbert with the metaphysicals; he belongs to them "only by virtue of qualities which in him are poetically secondary."

acceptance of Christian doctrine, might equally well engender a readiness to perceive relationships between apparently unlike objects. The first would do so because the faculties would be specially alert, and the intellect eager to try out various fancies in the hope of producing something new. The second would do so because Christianity commits a man to interpret everything in the light of paradoxes. The true metaphysical poets belong to the first class, George Herbert to the second.

There are some lines in Donne's poem *The Crosse* which illustrate precisely this Christian tendency to look out for analogies between the temporal and the eternal:

> Looke down, thou spiest out Crosses in small things;
> Looke up, thou seest birds rais'd on crossed wings.[1]

Yet the poem as a whole makes clear the difference between the metaphysical and the devout use of Christian symbolism. It opens with a moving quatrain:

> Since Christ embrac'd the Crosse it selfe, dare I
> His image, th' image of his Crosse deny?
> Would I have profit by the Sacrifice,
> And dare the chosen Altar to despise?

Soon, however, Donne is carried away by the paradoxical possibilities inherent in the idea of the Cross, and his conceits become progressively more extravagant, until we get such lines as these:

> And as the braine through bony walls doth vent
> By sutures, which a Crosses form present,
> So when thy braine workes, ere thou utter it,
> Crosse and correct concupiscence of wit.

[1] *Poetical Works*, ed. H. J. C. Grierson, 1912, vol. i. p. 331–333.

Literary Affinities

It seems a pity in this instance that Donne did not take his own advice, for we are finally more impressed by his mental agility than by his capacity to penetrate the mystery of the Cross. In the far finer and more passionate poem, *Good Friday 1613, Riding Westward*, we get a passage which is traditionally Christian in its symbolism but authentically metaphysical in expression.

> Could I behold those hands which span the Poles,
> And turne all spheares at once, pierc'd with those holes?
> Could I behold that endlesse height which is
> Zenith to us, and our Antipodes
> Humbled below us?[1]

These antitheses between the almightiness of God and the abject condition of Jesus crucified are essentially the same as those which Herbert uses so tellingly in *The Sacrifice*. He, however, presents them dramatically and ironically, without recourse to cosmographical allusions. Herbert relies far more than Donne on the power of a single image to evoke associations; it is less by unexpected juxtapositions that he achieves his witty effects than by the development of the various suggestions inherent in his symbols.

A consideration of his sonnet *Christmas* may throw some light on the way in which his imagination worked. The first quatrain is narrative in effect; Herbert here is using his favourite parable technique.

> All after pleasures as I rid one day,
>   My horse and I, both tir'd, body and minde,
>   With full crie of affections, quite astray,
>   I took up in the next inne I could finde.   (p. 80).

---

[1] *op. cit.* p. 336–337. One of the MSS adds to the title of the poem "Riding to Sir Edward Herbert in Wales."

George Herbert

The inn does not suggest, in the first instance, the lodging-house at Bethlehem, but simply a place of rest and refreshment.

> There when I came, whom found I but my deare,
> My dearest Lord, expecting till the grief
> Of pleasures brought me to him, readie there
> To be all passengers most sweet relief?

The idea of the Church as an inn occurs in medieval writers. St. Catherine of Siena in *A Treatise of Discretion* writes of the hostelry in the garden of Holy Church, which keeps and ministers the Bread of Life and gives to drink of the Blood, so that God's creatures, journeying on their pilgrimage, may not through weariness faint by the way.[1] Though Herbert's traveller is a huntsman, not a pilgrim, it is solace that he seeks; and Christ is simultaneously the host and the feast. In passing we may note that the idea behind the phrase "the grief of pleasure" resembles that in *The Pulley*:

> Let him be rich and wearie, that at least,
> If goodnesse lead him not, yet wearinesse
>   May tosse him to my breast. (p. 160).

The consideration of Christ's loving welcome to all travellers leads Herbert to contrast it with the harsh reception given to the Christ-child at Bethlehem:

> O Thou, whose glorious, yet contracted light,
> Wrapt in nights mantle, stole into a manger;
> Since my dark soul and brutish is thy right,
> To man of all beasts be not thou a stranger.

These lines stir up a complex of associations in anyone familiar

---

[1] *The Dialogues of S. Catherine of Siena,* tr. Algar Thorold, Kegan Paul, 1907.

Literary Affinities

with the Christmas story; the midnight birth in the stable, the cradling of the Son of God among the stalled beasts, the light of the world shining in the darkness that could neither eclipse nor comprehend it. "Glorious yet contracted light" might be called a scientific image, but it does not seduce Herbert into a disquisition on optics; the four words are all that he needs to suggest the willing assumption by the Godhead of human limitations. The thought of the stabled beasts calls up again the image in the first quatrain, "my horse and I, both tir'd, body and minde", and Herbert prays that his own brutishness, and Man's, may not be worse than that of the ox and ass:

> Furnish and decke my soul, that thou mayst have
> A better lodging then a rack or grave.

Now the associations of the inn are transferred to the human soul, which must be transformed into a fit dwelling-place for the Lord of Life. "Rack" suggests at once the manger and the instrument of torture, and perhaps it is the second meaning that calls up the word "grave". It is characteristic of Herbert that even a sonnet on Christmas should end on a note recalling the Passion.[1]

Leaving aside what may be called the Christian content of the poem, it is still an admirable work of art, the product of an uncommonly lively poetic intelligence. Herbert's economy in packing so many ideas into so small a compass, the subtlety with which he makes his transitions from one aspect of his subject to another, the sureness of his emotional control—these are all attributes of wit, and it is by virtue of this wit that his poems are so immeasurably superior to the average run of pious verse.

---

[1] In the draft in the Williams MS the poem concludes:
> ffurnish my soule to thee, yt being drest
> Of better lodging thou maist be possest.

George Herbert

His alert intelligence controls the expression of even his most poignant feelings. *The Crosse,* for example, is a heart-rending poem, yet it vibrates with intellectual energy, particularly the final verse:

> Ah my deare Father, ease my smart!
> These contrarieties crush me: these crosse actions
> Doe winde a rope about, and cut my heart:
> And yet since these thy contradictions
> Are properly a crosse felt by thy Sonne,
> With but four words, my words, *Thy will be done.*
>
> (p. 165).

The poem of lamentation comes to a heroic conclusion, and each stage of the change of mood can be followed out in these few lines. His own will has been crossed by God's, his heart cut cross-wise by frustrations. It is the image of the cross that brings home to him the true significance of his sufferings, and he is accordingly able to accept, as one of God's sons, his own minor crucifixion, and to make Christ's words his own.

Or we may take the last two stanzas of another moving poem, which is conspicuously witty throughout, *The Temper i.* Herbert, having begged God not to rack him with trials, concludes:

> Yet take thy way; for sure thy way is best:
> Stretch or contract me, thy poore debter:
> This is but tuning of my breast,
>   To make the musick better.
>
> Whether I flie with angels, fall with dust,
> Thy hands made both, and I am there:
> Thy power and love, my love and trust,
>   Make one place ev'ry where. (p. 55).

Herbert conceives of himself at first as an unprofitable servant, who deserves to be tortured upon the rack; but the thought of its cruel screws suggests the screws of the lute, which must tighten the strings to the appropriate tensions if the instrument is to be well tempered. (In *Easter*, the lute is compared to the cross, and its stretched strings with the sinews of the crucified, Christ's sufferings being in themselves a hymn of praise, and also the occasion for mankind to sing praises.) Having equated his heart with the lute, Herbert is able to take joy in his pains, for without them he would be as useless as an untuned instrument of music. In the final verse there is a reminder of the extremes of Man's destiny: "Thou hast made him a little lower than the angels, to crown him with glory and worship" —"Dust thou art, and unto dust shalt thou return." There is also an echo of Donne's lines:

> For love, all love of other sights controules,
> And makes one little roome, an ev'ry where. [1]

The allusions are fleetingly made, and Herbert sets his own unmistakable stamp upon the verse in the simple, concentrated second line: "Thy hands made both, and I am there." Before he actually mentions God's power and love, as he does in the following line, he calls them to mind; for God's hands are creative, fashioning all things, from celestial beings to the dust of the earth, and also sustaining, so that he can entrust himself to their keeping without any fear of coming to harm.

Herbert conveys an intensity of emotion by means of phrases charged with thought. His wit is one of his foremost qualities. But since this wit does not depend for its effect upon far-fetched conceits, recondite allusions or reasoned arguments, there seems to be no good reason for describing it as metaphysical, or for connecting it inseparably with the wit of Donne.

[1] *Poetical Works*, ed. Grierson, vol. i. p. 7.

VIII

The Christian Poet

THERE is one straightforward sense in which all the poetry of Herbert can be described as metaphysical. Not a single lyric in *The Temple* is addressed to a human being or written in honour of one. The love that inspired him to poetry was in the primary meaning of the word metaphysical. Yet one cannot stretch the word to include all devotional poetry, or it loses what little significance it still retains as a term of literary criticism.

Herbert was constantly concerned with the relation between the finite and the infinite, between the human and the divine; but his concern was practical. He wrote as a devoutly believing Christian, who strove for a closer knowledge of the God whom he worshipped and served. Theological subtleties did not interest him, though he studied divinity for years and lived in an age when points of doctrine were debated with passion even by the laity. Typically, he did not include in *The Temple* a poem on the Holy Communion which appears in the Williams MS and is a disquisition on eucharistic theories. Instead, he wrote a poem that emphasizes the simplicity of the means by which God conveys grace to the soul:

> Not in rich furniture, or fine array,
>   Not in a wedge of gold,
>   Thou, who for me wast sold,
> To me dost now thy self convey;
> For so thou should'st without me still have been,
>   Leaving within me sinne.

The Christian Poet

> But by the way of nourishment and strength
> Thou creep'st into my breast ... (p. 52).

It is the welfare of the soul that interests Herbert; he never tires of contemplating the ways in which God deals with his creatures; and as a priest he has a special concern with the means of grace entrusted to the church.

There are occasions when Herbert's disinclination to consider obvious metaphysical problems makes him appear a little smug. In his poem *Providence* he is so full of admiration for God's "curious art in marshalling (his) goods" that he omits all consideration of the waste and cruelty in nature. But possibly he really did believe that there was no waste; there is a quaint passage in *The Country Parson* that supports this notion. The parson "admires and imitates the wonderfull providence and thrift of the great householder of the world: for there being two things, which as they are, are unuseful to man, the one for smalnesse, as crums, and scattered corn, and the like; the other for the foulnesse, as wash, and durt, and things therinto fallen; God hath provided Creatures for both; for the first, Poultry; for the second, swine. These save men the labour, and doing that which either he could not do, or was not fit for him to do, by taking both sorts of food into them, do as it were dresse and prepare both for man in themselves, by growing themselves fit for his table" (p. 241).

Herbert's complete certainty that the economy of the world, of the universe, even, is geared to the requirements of man gives to some of his work an archaic flavour. Whereas Donne and Edward Herbert and Marvell, and even Vaughan, are indeed among those poets who, "aware of the difficulty of metaphysical problems, see them lurking behind every action, however trivial",[1] George Herbert took for granted one

[1] James Smith, *On Metaphysical Poetry*, reprinted from *Scrutiny* in *Discriminations*, Chatto & Windus, 1934.

complete and stupendous set of assumptions, basing his thinking and his behaviour on them. His consciousness of the inter-relations of time and eternity, visible and invisible, mortal and immortal, differs from that of the genuine metaphysical poets in being founded on an extraordinarily assured and unquestioning faith. He really did believe in the Incarnation and its consequences, so that his whole interpretation of the world was bound to be in sacramental terms. The paradoxes of Christianity were constantly in his mind, but they did not present themselves as problems.

It would indeed be strange if a Christian poet did not ponder on the tensions created by such inseparable contraries as human and divine, physical and spiritual. Many of Herbert's poems are clearly the fruit of such pondering. *Mortification* is concerned with the double-faceted fact of life and death, *Man's Medley* with the contrast between here and hereafter, and with man's dual nature. But Herbert does not present these contraries as though they constituted difficulties. For him all contraries were appointed elements in a divinely organized scheme. Christianity was, to Herbert, something absolutely given; a revealed religion, not a tenable philosophy. The only problems that racked him, if we may judge from the poems, were emotional, not intellectual. "Will great God measure with a wretch?" he cries, or exclaims, "Thou dost deign/To enter combat with us", or

> There thou art struggling with a peevish heart,
> Which sometimes crosseth thee, thou sometimes it:
> The fight is hard on either part . . .
>
> (*Sion*, p. 106).

Believing, as he did, that God is Love, he was naturally bound to suffer anguish of spirit when, through no wilful fault of his own, he felt himself alienated; and the problem

The Christian Poet

of why his all-powerful and all-loving Master should refuse to relieve him was a torture. Not philosophy, but faith, is required to show the way out of this dilemma.

Herbert's mind operated in the sphere of faith, and he was therefore able to accept, and rejoice in, many dualities which a truly metaphysical mind might have sought to resolve. The acceptance of the Christian scheme did not at all hamper the play of his imagination, but rather liberated it, for Christianity is a profoundly poetic religion.

Its central thesis, that God became Man, is the paradox beyond which thought cannot go; and the story of Jesus makes the paradox wilder still, since it shows the Son of God scorned, misunderstood and rejected by his chosen people, yet finally triumphant over death itself. The gospel story is much enriched by the store of Hebrew prophecy and poetry that preceded it; and the early fathers of the church took a delight in counterpointing the biblical themes and heightening every similarity and contrast suggested by the scriptures.

In the most ancient Christian hymns there is a combination of wit and devotion that is very similar to what we find in Herbert's poetry. In *A solis ortus cardine,* written in the middle of the fifth century, we get the conceit that he whose bounty feeds all creation is himself fed at Mary's breast, and the Good Shepherd is revealed to the shepherds of Bethlehem. In *Hostis Herodes impie,* a hymn of the same period, we find a series of neat and telling paradoxes. Two verses from Dr. Percy Dearmer's translation[1] may be quoted, since they prove how ancient is the tradition of epigrammatic and witty sacred verse.

> The Lamb of God is manifest
> Again in Jordan's water blest,
> And he who sin had never known
> By washing hath our sins undone.

[1] *English Hymnal,* no. 38.

George Herbert

> Yet he that ruleth everything
> Can change the nature of the spring,
> And gives at Cana this for sign—
> The water reddens into wine.

The two hymns written in honour of the Holy Cross by Venantius Fortunatus in the sixth century are magnificent examples of Christian poetry by a man whose heart and mind were equally engaged in his writing; and the transformation of the cross from a gallows to a "tree of beauty, tree of light" is in itself an example of the way in which the church over the centuries, enriches all her symbols.

Although the Latin office hymns of the Sarum use were no longer, in Herbert's day, used at morning and evening prayer, he was undoubtedly familiar with them, and with the hymns of medieval devotion. In *The Sacrifice,* perhaps the finest of all his poems in its sustained pathos and irony, he is far nearer to the Catholic liturgy than to any contemporary poetic model. The wit there displayed is not "metaphysical", it is intrinsically Christian.

Pascal, a generation younger than Herbert, never tires of reiterating in his *Pensées* the essentially contradictory nature of the Christian religion. This, he says, "properly consists in the mystery of the Redeemer, who, uniting in Himself the two natures, human and divine, has redeemed men from the corruption of sin in order to reconcile them in His divine person to God. The Christian religion, then, teaches men these two truths; that there is a God whom men can know, and that there is a corruption in their nature which renders them unworthy of Him".[1]

Herbert grasped this dual truth with complete assurance. The theme appears again and again in his writings, most often as the tension between Love and Sin. His sensitive intelli-

---

[1] Everyman's Library edition, p. 152.

gence assimilated the teachings of the Church and at the same time digested his experiences in the world of affairs and learning. It is the combination of piety and a genuine knowledge of human nature that equips Herbert so singularly well for the writing of Christian poetry; and to this must be added his acute insight into his own self.

Without self-knowledge, and the humility that follows on relentless scrutiny of his own motives, a man should not undertake to write religious verse. Herbert felt himself morally bound to avoid insincerity. He neither faked nor inflated his emotions, and this basic honesty strengthens the whole fabric of his poetry. He expressed his religious feelings and convictions in workaday language, a soundly Christian practice, though it may seem odd to people accustomed to regard religion as something sacrosanct. Herbert did not take a portentously solemn attitude either towards God or towards his own sins and shortcomings, nor find it necessary to pitch his voice in a sanctimonious key when he spoke of God's love. It was a daily experience, and could therefore be treated in the language of every day.

Nothing that we know of Herbert suggests that he had in him any trace of that exhibitionism which made Donne dress up in his shroud and have his effigy sketched while he was still alive. Nevertheless, he was deeply and incessantly interested in his own psychology, anatomizing his every mood and scrutinizing his motives with a subtlety not inferior to Donne's. He did not condone the weaknesses he discovered, but neither did he wallow in remorse. Even towards his own intractable heart he could be patient and tolerant.

In every sense of the word, Herbert was humane. His letters, Walton's anecdotes, and above all *The Country Parson* testify to his courtesy and, in his latter years, his loving-kindness. Accustomed from childhood to move at ease among cultivated people, in circles where the arts were practised and

George Herbert

learning honoured, he acquired the poised and easy manner that is an agreeable mark of good breeding; and when he turned his back on the great world, he was no less at home among the country folk of his little parish. If there is an element of condescension in the attitude of the parson to his rural neighbours, it is not based on any false assumption of innate superiority, but on an honest recognition that he, as a gentleman and scholar, has enjoyed advantages, and that these advantages impose great obligations.

Outside the sphere of personal relationships, Herbert is equally civilized. His avoidance of theological controversy, most remarkable considering the epoch in which he lived, is based on a genuine spirit of religious tolerance. The country parson "doth assure himself, that God in all ages hath had his servants, to whom he hath revealed his truth as well as to him; and that as one Countrey doth not bear all things, that there may be a Commerce; so neither hath God opened, or will open, all to one, that there may be a traffick in knowledge between the servants of God, for the planting both of love, and humility" (p. 229).

Although he imposed upon himself, at Bemerton, strict rules of mortification, there is no sign whatever in his writings of a kill-joy puritan spirit. The gracefulness with which he rejected the "world of sugred lies" implied no harsh censure on those who still felt its attractions.

> If then all that worldlings prize
>   Be contracted to a rose;
> Sweetly there indeed it lies,
>   But it biteth in the close.
>
> So this flower doth judge and sentence
>   Wordly joyes to be a scourge:
> For they all produce repentance,
>   And repentance is a purge.

The Christian Poet

> But I health, not physick choose:
>   Onely though I you oppose,
> Say that fairly I refuse,
>   For my answer is a rose.
> (The Rose, p. 178).

Though Herbert believed this mortal life to be only the prelude to a fuller existence, he did not underestimate the worth of the good things that the present world affords; learning, honour, social pleasures, music, poetry, the pleasures of the senses, all these things were to him the foretaste of more substantial joys:

> For as thou dost impart thy grace,
>   The greater shall our glorie be.
> The measure of our joyes is in this place,
>   The stuffe with thee.
> (Employment i, p. 57).

His upbringing had happily kept him free from the scruples that beset so many strenuously righteous people in the seventeenth century. The son of Magdalen Herbert, the brother of the Master of the Revels, did not need the reassurance that Donne in one of his sermons gave to his congregation: "Fear not thou, that a chearefulnesse and alacrity in using God's blessings, feare not that a moderate delight in musique, in conversation, in recreations, shall be imputed to thee for a fault, for it is conceived by the Holy Ghost, and is the off-spring of a peaceful conscience."[1]

The tranquillity that does, in spite of many poems of distress, underlie the writings of Herbert springs from his conviction that God, by condescending to man's estate, hallowed the whole of human life, and by suffering on man's behalf made even pain intelligible. This certainty saved him from

[1] Sermon, xxxvi.

George Herbert

narrowness of sympathy towards his fellow-men and from morbidity in his own spiritual life.

A line from *The Rose,* recently quoted, is pathetic when we consider that it was written only a short time before he was assailed by a mortal illness:

> But I health, not physick, choose.

It is strictly true, however, when we compare the sane temper of Herbert's religious lyrics with even such fine but fevered devotional verse as Crashaw's. It is significant that the most poignant and grief-stricken poems in *The Temple* are immediately followed by poems of affirmation and hope. It cannot be fortuitous that the opening line of *The Bag,* "Away despair! my gracious Lord doth heare" should follow the heart-broken plaints of *Longing,* nor that *The Crosse* should be counterbalanced by *The Flower,* with its buoyant opening, "How fresh, O Lord, how sweet and clean/Are thy returns!" If Herbert was tempted at times to indulge in an excess of melancholy, his sober grasp of the true situation soon reasserted itself. God's ways may be past understanding, but his wisdom overrules all. Because Herbert genuinely believed this, he could dare to say:

> Thy will such a strange distance is,
>   As that to it
> East and West touch, the poles do kisse,
>   And parallels meet.
>   (*The Search,* p. 163).

He can nevertheless conclude this poem, which laments his utter alienation from God, with the confident assertion

>   For as thy absence doth excell
>   All distance known,
> So doth thy nearenesse bear the bell,
>   Making two one.

The Christian Poet

This sanity is one of the qualities that endears Herbert to English readers, who admire signs of good health more readily than they find invalids interesting.

During the seventeenth century, and indeed until the Augustan critics put all poets of his generation into eclipse, Herbert's poems were widely read and much admired. *The Temple* went into four editions within three years, and it was steadily reprinted until 1709. No doubt it was their piety, rather than their literary originality, that commended the poems to the majority of readers, but they had an extraordinarily kindling effect upon poets when they fell into their hands.

Richard Crashaw named his own first volume of sacred verse *Steps to the Temple,* and included in it some verses "On Mr. G. Herbert's booke sent to a Gentlewoman", of which the opening quatrain runs:

> Know you, faire, on what you looke;
> Divinest love lyes in this booke:
> Expecting fire from your eyes
> To kindle this his sacrifice.[1]

Anything more offensive to Herbert than the implication of the second couplet can scarcely be imagined.

> Doth Poetry
> Wear *Venus* Livery? only serve her turn?
> Why are not *Sonnets* made of thee? and layes
> Upon thine Altar burnt? (p. 206).

But Crashaw was always liable to lapses of taste, especially where the distinction between sacred and profane love is involved. The chief link between the two poets was the household at Little Gidding, where the Ferrars cherished the reputation of George Herbert both as poet and saint. Crashaw

[1] *Poetical Works,* ed. L. C. Martin, Oxford, 1927, p. 130.

frequently visited them during his years at Cambridge, and *The Temple* may have provided the impetus that turned his poetic gifts in the direction of sacred verse. His poems owe nothing discernible to Herbert's example, but the fact remains that he paid homage to him by giving to his own collection of sacred lyrics a title suggesting its inferiority to *The Temple*.

Henry Vaughan was by his own confession inspired to the writing of religious lyrics by George Herbert's "holy life and verse". He borrowed from *The Temple* to such an extent that his own originality is sometimes impaired, but it was all done in the spirit of a humble and grateful convert, readily acknowledging his indebtedness to "a most glorious true Saint, and a Seer". Vaughan was himself perhaps more of a seer than Herbert, but had he not felt himself much inferior as an artist he would scarcely have leant so heavily on the poems in *The Temple*.

Among lesser men, Christopher Harvey has already been mentioned on account of his book, first published anonymously in 1640, entitled *The Synagogue, or, The Shadow of The Temple,* on which he endeavoured to fill up some of the gaps left in George Herbert's collected poems. In case anyone should miss the significance of the title, there is the acknowledgment "In imitation of Mr. George Herbert", and a translation of a motto from Pliny's Epistles, "Not to imitate the best examples is the greatest folly". A comparison of the 1640 edition of *The Synagogue* with the much enlarged version of 1661 shows that it was indeed the imitation of Herbert that redeemed Harvey's verse from prosy didacticism.[1]

---

[1] He does, however, deserve fame for his wonderful epigram in *Schola Cordis*, 1647:

> The whole round earth is not enough to fill
>   The heart's three corners, but it craveth still.
> Only the Trinity, that made it, can
>   Suffice the vast three-cornered heart of man.

The Christian Poet

Canon Hutchinson's introduction to Herbert's *Works* includes an interesting section on Herbert's contemporary and later reputation, and it is not necessary to recapitulate it here; but nobody interested in assessing his poetic merits should overlook the fact that his known admirers include people of such differing tastes as Charles I, Richard Baxter the puritan divine, Henry Purcell, Cromwell's chaplain Peter Sterry, John Wesley (who modified a number of his poems for use in methodist hymnals), William Cowper, S. T. Coleridge, Gerard Manley Hopkins and Aldous Huxley.

It was Coleridge who rediscovered Herbert's value as a poet after he had been neglected for a long period. Besides his notes to Pickering's edition of Herbert's works, there is his often-quoted verdict that appeared as a note to Essay VI of the first volume of *The Friend*: "Having mentioned the name of Herbert, that model of a man, a gentleman and a clergyman, let me add that the quaintness of some of his thoughts (not of his diction, than which nothing can be more pure, manly and unaffected) has blinded modern readers to the great general merit of his poems, which are for the most part exquisite of their kind." Coleridge also wrote to the Royal Academician, Collins: "I find more substantial comfort now in pious George Herbert's *Temple,* which I used to read to amuse myself with his quaintness, in short, only to laugh at, than in all the poetry since the poetry of Milton. If you have not read Herbert I can recommend the book to you confidently. The *poem* entitled *The Flower* is especially affecting, and to me such a phrase as '*and relish versing*' expresses a sincerity and reality, which I would unwillingly exchange for the more dignified '*and once more love the Muse*' etc., and so with many other of Herbert's homely phrases."[1]

During the nineteenth century many popular editions and selections of Herbert's poems were published, which re-

---

[1] *Essays and Lectures on Shakespeare and some other old poets and dramatists.*

George Herbert

established him as a devotional writer, even if critics still felt obliged to apologize for his oddities of expression.

Today Herbert's reputation is higher than it has been since the end of the seventeenth century. He has been borne forward on the wave of critical admiration that has carried Donne and Marvell, Crashaw and Vaughan and a number of lesser writers out of the obscurity which so long engulfed them. Thanks to various critics and teachers who have laboured over the last thirty years to analyse the peculiar merits of metaphysical poetry, we are again able to approach the poets of Herbert's epoch in the confident expectation of enjoyment and with a reasonably good apparatus for understanding them.

It is, however, wise to guard against the mistake of seeing only those qualities which we are on the look-out for. Herbert has a good many of the characteristics which we associate with the Donne tradition, but others, more fundamental, mark him out as a poet of great literary discrimination who went his own way. His untroubled acceptance of Christian orthodoxy, according to the tenets of the church into which he was born, gives the whole of his poetry a bias towards simplicity which is not characteristic of the metaphysicals.

This simplicity of spirit perhaps explains why Herbert's name is cherished by a number of people who care little about contemporary currents in literary criticism, or, for that matter, about other seventeenth-century poets. They associate Herbert with the best traditions of the Anglican church, and remember particularly those of his poems which are in use as hymns. There are not many of these; but the seventeenth century, in spite of producing so much good devotional verse, did not bequeath much that is suitable for congregational singing. Herbert's version of the 23rd psalm, his "Let all the world in every corner sing", his "King of glory, king of peace" and "Teach me, my God and King" keep his memory alive among many who have few literary pretensions.

The Christian Poet

Herbert's common sense and tender sensibility, his moderation, courtesy and stubborn honesty, make an amalgam that is conspicuously English; and his language, too, defies translation in its colloquial richness and ease. His concern with ethics rather than dogma commends him to his fellow-countrymen, and so does his power of maintaining an equilibrium in emotional storms.

All these considerations help to account for the affectionate regard in which his readers hold George Herbert; but the simplest explanation of his ability to endear himself to us is that his writings reveal him as an exceptionally lovable man. *The Temple* is, ultimately, a spiritual autobiography. Herbert himself described it as "a picture of the many spiritual Conflicts that have past betwixt God and my Soul", and asked Nicholas Ferrar to make it public only "if he can think it may turn to the advantage of any dejected poor Soul ... if not, let him burn it". Into the poems Herbert put all his preoccupations; his anxieties, his hopes, his consciousness of failure, his thankfulness; not with any intention whatever of bequeathing a self-portrait to posterity, but in an endeavour to raise

> A broken Altar ...
> Made of a heart, and cemented with teares;
> Whose parts are as thy hand did frame ...
> *(The Altar,* p. 26).

In a lesser degree, *A Priest to the Temple* is also a mirror in which we can discern the features of George Herbert. The two books, though their author did not so intend them, do in fact enable us to know him as intimately as we know our friends; and knowing him, it is impossible not to love him.

Select Bibliography

AUBREY, JOHN. *Brief Lives,* ed. O. Lawson Dick, Secker & Warburg, 1949.

BEACHCROFT, T. O. *Nicholas Ferrar: his influence on and friendship with George Herbert. The Criterion* xii, 1932.

BEECHING, H. C. *George Herbert's Country Parson.* Blackwell, 1898 (an edition, with introduction, of *A Priest to the Temple,* reprinted 1916). *Religio Medici,* Smith, Elder, 1902.

BENNETT, J. *Four Metaphysical Poets,* Cambridge U.P., 1934.

BLACKSTONE, B. *The Ferrar Papers,* Cambridge U. P., 1938.

BLUNDEN, E. *George Herbert's Latin Poems, Essays & Studies of the English Association,* xix, 1934.

BUSH, D. *English Literature in the Earlier Seventeenth Century, 1600–1666,* Clarendon Press, 1945.

CLARK, G. N. *The Seventeenth Century,* Clarendon Press, 1929.

CROPPER, M. *Flame touches Flame,* Longmans, 1949.

DONNE, JOHN. *Poetical Works,* ed. H. J. C. Grierson, Clarendon Press, 1912. *Sermon preached at the Obsequies of Lady Danvers,* London, 1627.

DOWDEN, E. *Puritan and Anglican,* Kegan Paul, 1900.

ELIOT, T. S. *The Metaphysical Poets* in *Selected Essays,* Faber, 1932. Articles on Herbert in *The Spectator* (12, iii. 32), and *Times Literary Supplement* (2. iii. 33).

EMPSON, W. *Seven Types of Ambiguity,* pp. 286–95. Chatto & Windus, 1930.

FREEMAN, R. *English Emblem Books,* Chatto & Windus, 1948.

Select Bibliography

GARDNER, H. Edition of *Donne's Sacred Poems*, Clarendon Press, 1950.

GARROD, H. W. *Donne & Mrs. Herbert*, Review of English Studies, xxi, 1945.

GRIERSON, H. J. C. Edition of *Donne's Poetical Works*, Clarendon Press, 1912. *Metaphysical Poetry, Donne to Butler*, 1925. *Cross-Currents in English Literature of the Seventeenth Century*, Chatto & Windus, 1929.

HARVEY, CHRISTOPHER. *The Synagogue*, London, 1640.

HERBERT, EDWARD (Baron Herbert of Cherbury), *Autobiography*, ed. Sidney Lee, revised edn., Routledge, 1906. *Poems*, ed. G. E. Moore Smith, Clarendon Press, 1923.

HERBERT, GEORGE. Besides the early editions of his works referred to in the text, and the two big editions by F. E. Hutchinson and G. H. Palmer, I have referred to the Nonesuch Edition of *The Temple*, ed. Francis Meynell, 1927, and the Everyman's Library edition of *The Temple and A Priest to the Temple*, ed. Edward Thomas, 1927.

HUTCHINSON, F. E. Edition of *The Works of George Herbert*, Clarendon Press, 1941. *George Herbert*, in *Seventeenth-Century Studies presented to Sir Herbert Grierson*, Oxford, 1938. Chapter in *C.H.E.L.* vol. vii, on *The Sacred Poets*.

HUTTON, W. H. Chapter in *C.H.E.L.* vol. vii. on *Caroline Divines*.

HYDE, A. G. *George Herbert and his Times*, Methuen, 1906.

KNIGHTS, L. C. *George Herbert*, article in *Scrutiny*, xii, 1944.

LEAVIS, F. R. *The Line of Wit*, in *Revaluation*, Chatto & Windus, 1936.

LEE, S. Edition of Lord Herbert's *Autobiography*, revised edn., Routledge, 1906.

LEISHMAN, J. B. *The Metaphysical Poets*, Clarendon Press, 1934.

MAHOOD, M. M. *Poetry and Humanism*, Cape, 1950.

MATHEW, D. *The Jacobean Age*, Longmans, 1938.

Select Bibliography

PALMER, G. H. Edition of *The English Works of George Herbert*, 3rd edn., Houghton Mifflin, 1915.

PRAZ, M. *Studies in Seventeenth-Century Imagery*, vol. iii of *Studies of the Warburg Institute*, 1939. *La poesia metafisica inglese del seicento*, Rome, 1945.

SMITH, J. *On Metaphysical Poetry*, reprinted from *Scrutiny* in *Determinations*, Chatto & Windus, 1934.

SPENCER, T. (editor). *A Garland for John Donne*, Harvard U.P., 1931. *Studies in Metaphysical Poetry* (with Mark Van Doren), Columbia U.P., 1939.

TILLYARD, E. M. W. *The Elizabethan World Picture*, Chatto & Windus, 1943.

TUVE, R. *A Reading of George Herbert*, Faber, 1952.

WALTON, IZAAK. *The Lives of Dr. John Donne, Sir Henry Wotton, Mr. George Herbert* . . . London, 1670. *Lives*, ed. G. Saintsbury, World's Classics, 1927.

WHITE, H. *English Devotional Literature*, University of Wisconsin Studies, 1931. *The Metaphysical Poets*, N. Y. & Macmillan, 1936.

WILLEY, B. *The Seventeenth-Century Background*, Chatto & Windus, 1934.

WILLIAMSON, G. *The Donne Tradition*, Harvard U.P., 1930.

WILSON, F. P. *Elizabethan and Jacobean*, Clarendon Press, 1945.

Index

Andrewes, Lancelot, 16, 56, 68
Aubrey, John, 9, 10 n., 14, 26, 30, 34, 41, 47, 57 n.

Bacon, Lord Chancellor, 9, 17, 18, 21, 49, 55
Bath and Wells, 29
Baxter, Richard, 47, 145
Baynton House, 26, 33
Bemerton, 3, 22, 29, 30, 31, 33, 34, 36, 37, 39, 40, 41, 42, 43, 47, 51, 55, 56, 67, 70, 73, 74, 120, 140
Black Hall, 5
Blake, William, 85, 92
Blunden, Edmund, 24
Bostock, Nathaniel, 34, 39, 46
Boswell, William, 18
Browne, Sir Thomas, 72
Buck, Thomas, 50
Buckingham, Duke of, 21
Bunyan, John, 76

Calvin, Jean, 81
Cambridge, 2, 9, 10-18, 21, 26, 36, 49, 50, 55, 56, 73, 101
   King's College, 17
   Trinity College, 9, 11, 12, 17, 120
Campion, Thomas, 104, 106, 124
Catherine of Siena, Saint, 130
Charles I, 14, 16, 17, 29, 30, 47, 145

Chelsea, 9, 19
Chippenham, 25
Clifford, Lady Anne, 39
Coleridge, S. T., 109, 145
Collins, William, 145
Condell, Henry, 14
Cook, Sir Robert, 47
Cornaro, Luigi, 37, 55
Cotton, Charles, 13
Coventry and Lichfield, 9
Cowper, William, 145
Cranmer, Thomas, 68
Crashaw, Richard, 142, 143-4, 146
Creighton, Robert, 56
Cromwell, Oliver, 52, 145
Curll, Walter, 29

Danby, Earl of, 9, 24, 25, 26
Daniel, Roger, 50
Dante Alighieri, 85
Danvers, Jane, 26-7, 33, 46
Danvers, Sir John, 6, 9, 12, 13, 19, 119 n.
Danvers, Thomas, 47
Dauntsey House, 25, 26
Davenant, John, 30, 31
Dearmer, Percy, 137
Donne, John, 1, 4, 6, 7, 8, 16, 19, 20, 23, 29, 33, 49, 58, 59, 73, 84, 100, 103, 104, 107, 117-19, 121, 123, 126, 127, 128-9, 133, 135, 139, 141, 146

Index

Dorset, Earl of, 39
Dowland, John, 124
Duncon, Edmond, 36, 40, 46, 50, 51, 52, 54

Earle, John, 67
Edington, 26
Elizabeth I, 69
Empson, William, 91 n.
Eyton, 5

Ferrar, John, 35
Ferrar, Nicholas, 31, 35, 36, 37, 40, 50, 51, 52, 55, 56, 57, 69, 70, 143, 147
Ferrar, Susanna, 51
Freeman, Rosemary, 111–12
Fugglestone St. Peter, 29

Garthwait, Timothy, 52
Grierson, Sir Herbert, 88

Hacket, John, 9
Hamilton, Marquis of, 16
Harvey, Christopher, 61-2, 144
Heminge, John, 14
Henrietta Maria, 17
Henry, Prince of Wales, 49
Herbert, Charles, 8, 11, 22
Herbert, Edward, Lord Herbert of Cherbury, 5, 6, 15, 17, 18, 21, 22–3, 32, 41, 47, 69, 84, 104, 106, 115, 118, 124–7, 129 n., 135
Herbert, Elizabeth, 21
Herbert, Frances, 21
Herbert, Sir Henry, 15, 17, 21, 22, 23, 34, 35, 141

Herbert, Jane. *See* Danvers, Jane.
Herbert, Magdalen, 5, 6, 7, 8, 19, 20, 21, 23, 24, 38, 49, 101, 117, 120, 141
Herbert, Margaret, 22
Highnam House, 47
Hilliard, Nicholas, 1
Hooker, Richard, 26, 68
Hopkins, Gerard Manley, 66, 95–7, 145
Huntingdon, 51
Hutchinson, F. E., 9 n., 48 n., 52, 55, 58
Hutchinson, Mrs. Lucy, 16
Huxley, Aldous, 135

Ireland, Richard, 8, 9

Jackson, Thomas, 56
James I, 2, 12, 13, 14, 16, 17, 18, 70, 120
Jones, John, 51
Jonson, Ben, 118–19

Keble, John, 62
King, Henry, 106

Laud, William, 30, 71, 76
Law, William, 98
Leighton, 20, 34–6, 56
Lenox, Duke of, 35
Lessius, Leonard, 55
Lincoln, 20, 21, 56
Little Gidding, 31, 35, 36, 40, 50, 51, 69, 143
London, 6, 13, 17, 19, 21, 51, 52, 73
Luther, Martin, 81

Index

Mapletoft, Hugh, 51
Marvell, Andrew, 106, 135, 146
Mary I, 69
Maxey, T., 52
Mede, Joseph, 58
Melville, Andrew, 49
Milton, John, 32, 69, 91, 92, 106, 145
Montgomery Castle, 5
Montgomeryshire, 20
More, Sir Thomas, 19, 68

Nadder, river, 34
Nethersole, Sir Francis, 13, 15
New England, 81
Newmarket, 14
Newport, Lady, 5, 6, 38
Newton, Sir Isaac, 85

Oley, Barnabas, 29, 32, 35, 37, 43, 52, 53, 54
Oxford, 5, 6
  Bodleian Library, 50
  Corpus Christi College, 56
  New College, 11, 22
  University College, 5

Padua, 55
Palmer, G. H., 106
Paris, 15, 17
Parker, Matthew, 68
Pascal, Blaise, 86, 138
Pembroke, Countess of. *See* Sidney, Lady Mary.
Pembroke, Henry, Earl of, 119
Pembroke, Philip, Earl of, 14, 39, 120
Pembroke, William, 1st Earl of, 26

Pembroke, William, 3rd Earl of, 14, 15, 28, 29, 30, 39, 120
Pickering, William, 145
Pope, Alexander, 83
Purcell, Henry, 145

Raleigh, Sir Walter, 118
Rede, Sir Robert, 12
Richmond, Duke of, 16
Rome, English College, 69
Royston, 14

Salisbury, 3, 22, 29, 30, 31, 42, 47
Sancroft, William, 50 n.
Shakespeare, William, 14, 76
Sidney, Lady Mary, 14, 30, 119
Sidney, Sir Philip, 1, 14, 103, 118, 119, 120–4
Spenser, Edmund, 18, 92, 101, 113
Sterry, Peter, 145

Tennyson, Alfred, Lord, 106
Thorndyke, Herbert, 17
Traherne, Thomas, 86
Trollope, Anthony, 76
Tuve, Rosemond, 91 n., 93, 110
Twisse, William, 58

Valdesso, John, 36, 56
Vaughan, Henry, 86, 135, 144, 146
Venantius Fortunatus, 138

Walton, Izaak, 5, 6, 7, 8, 11, 13 n., 14, 15, 16, 19, 21, 25, 26, 27, 29, 30, 31, 32, 33, 35, 40, 41, 42, 43, 46, 47, 49, 54, 55, 56, 70, 101, 104, 139

Index

Wesley, John, 145
Westminster, 31
Westminster School, 8, 9, 17, 49
Winchester College, 8
Williams (Dr.) Library, 51

Wilton, 14, 26, 29, 30, 39, 120
Woodford, 21, 23, 55
Woodnoth, Arthur, 26, 30, 31, 35, 36, 46, 51, 52, 54
Wyatt, Sir Thomas, 104, 119